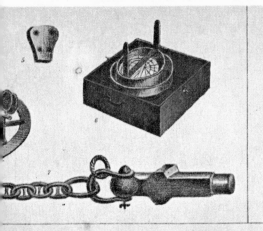

5. Large Cleat   6. Compass   7. Chain Cable.

Merry Christmas to Jam Jr.
from Aunt Barbara - Co
Dec. 1960

rd	21. Mizen top mast	26. Mizen top gall.t yard.
sail yard	22. Mizen top gall.t mast	27. Mizen royal yard.
gallant yard	23. Mizen royal mast	28. Gaff.
al yard	24. Cross jack yard	29. Stem.
ast	25. Mizen top yard	30. Stern.

TATES NAVY WARSHIP, 1815-1860.

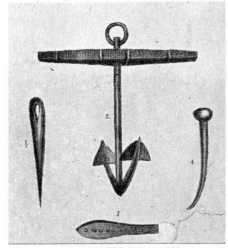

MARLIN SPIKES AND ANCHOR

STEPHEN DECATUR

THOMAS MACDONOUGH

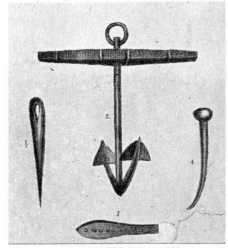

Six new AMERICAN HERITAGE JUNIOR LIBRARY books are published each year. Titles currently available are:

NAVAL BATTLES AND HEROES
THOMAS JEFFERSON AND HIS WORLD
DISCOVERERS OF THE NEW WORLD
RAILROADS IN THE DAYS OF STEAM
INDIANS OF THE PLAINS
THE STORY OF YANKEE WHALING

USS Arizona Memorial

COVER: America's *Constitution,* commanded by Captain Isaac Hull, winning her famous victory over the British frigate *Guerrière,* commanded by Captain James Dacres, off the coast at Halifax, Nova Scotia, on August 19, 1812.

TITLE PAGE: The frigate *United States,* commanded by Commodore John Barry, followed the custom of the day in displaying the flags of all the nations of the world at her launching ceremony in the Delaware River in 1797.

NAVAL BATTLES AND HEROES

ILLUSTRATED WITH PAINTINGS, PRINTS, DRAWINGS, MAPS AND PHOTOGRAPHS OF THE PERIOD

ND HEROES

BY THE EDITORS OF
AMERICAN HERITAGE

NARRATIVE BY
WILBUR CROSS

IN CONSULTATION WITH
REAR ADMIRAL
JOHN B. HEFFERNAN, U.S.N.
VICE PRESIDENT AND SECRETARY
NAVAL HISTORICAL FOUNDATION
WASHINGTON, D. C.

PUBLISHED BY
AMERICAN HERITAGE
PUBLISHING CO., INC.
NEW YORK

BOOK TRADE DISTRIBUTION BY
GOLDEN PRESS · NEW YORK

FOREWORD

The influence of naval events on American history has often been overlooked or misunderstood. For example, every account of the American Revolution records the important captures of the British armies of Burgoyne and Cornwallis, but frequently there is no mention of the decisive naval events which made those impressive victories possible.

The foresight of Washington, Schuyler, and Arnold provided a few small armed vessels on Lake Champlain in the spring of 1776. When pursuing British troops reached the lake, in their attempt to cut off New England and take New York City, they first had to build fighting vessels to destroy the American ships. Although the Americans were defeated, on October 12, 1776, as described in this volume, they had delayed the British invasion for a year, by which time Washington had assembled an army strong enough to stop Burgoyne.

Burgoyne's capture caused the King of France to ally himself with the colonists, and in 1781 to send a fleet to prevent the British Navy from rescuing the army of Cornwallis, which was hemmed in by Washington. The superior French fleet of Admiral de Grasse made the surrender at Yorktown inevitable.

The naval events leading to the capture of Burgoyne and Cornwallis, and many other fascinating operations of American seamen, are recounted in this book. The editors of American Heritage have been unable to record all of the battles and all of the courageous deeds of the heroes of the Navy, but they have selected battles— from the Revolution, the War of 1812, the Mexican and Civil Wars, and from World Wars I and II—which illustrate many climactic moments in United States naval history.

In this book, a narration of events is amplified by the reproduction of carefully chosen contemporary drawings, paintings, prints, photographs, and other illustrations, which add to the authentic flavor of the whole work.

The editors hope that young readers will here acquire an understanding of the great achievements and traditions of the United States Navy, as well as a desire to read further in its history.

—JOHN B. HEFFERNAN

FIRST EDITION

LIBRARY OF CONGRESS CATALOGUE CARD NUMBER: 60–13854

Fort Severn, built by the Army in 1809 to guard against the British, stood for 100 years at Annapolis, Maryland. Given to the Navy for use as the "Naval School" in 1845, it became the first building of the U.S. Naval Academy.

CONTENTS

THIS AMERICAN NAVAL FLAG WAS FLOWN ABOARD THE NEW FRIGATE "ALLIANCE" IN 1779.

PINE TREE FLAG OF THE FLOATING BATTERIES GUARDING PHILADELPHIA IN 1775.

IN 1779, JOHN PAUL J[ONES] FLEW THIS FLAG ABOARD [THE] CAPTURED FRIGATE "SERA[PIS."]

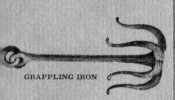

GRAPPLING IRON

QUADRANT

SEXTANT

ANCHOR

COILED ROPE

THIS SILHOUETTE OF YOUNG SENIOR LIEUTENANT JOHN PAUL JONES WAS MADE IN 1776.

IN 1776, CHRISTOPHER GADSDEN GAVE THIS FLAG TO THE CONTINENTAL NAVY.

COMMODORE ESEK HOPKINS FLEW THIS FIRST NAVY JACK ABOARD THE "ALFRED."

The First American Navy

"There she is! Board her, men!"

The little seaport town of Machias, Maine, echoed with the cries of stout Yankee seamen, thirty-five strong, at dawn on June 12, 1775, as they descended on the wharves and headed for the small merchant sloop *Unity* anchored nearby. Leading them was the lithe figure of one Jeremiah O'Brien, a determined Maine "Down-Easter." And the reason for the occasion was that word of the battles of Lexington and Concord had reached this northern New England outpost. The object of their attack was a Britisher, which had arrived to unload badly needed food supplies as a bribe for obtaining lumber for British-held Boston.

As O'Brien and his men swarmed over the *Unity*, the first real sea fight of the American Revolution began.

With the sloop captured, the Americans headed out into the harbor, where they quickly engaged the British armed cutter *Margaretta* in battle. It was a short, furious fight, with the British under one Midshipman Moore putting up stubborn resistance. The *Margaretta* had four three-pounders, but, not being able to bring them properly to bear in time, found herself locked with the *Unity* for hand-to-hand combat. The British helmsman was killed, and all resistance collapsed as the Americans clubbed their way aboard.

This was not the first time British ships had been set upon. In 1769 patriots at Newport had boarded and burned the British customs ship *Liberty;* and in 1772 another British customs vessel, the *Gaspée,* had been similarly destroyed in Narragansett Bay. But the Machias affair was the first real fight, and the first to occur after the Revolution had officially started. At the time, America had no navy. But she was a maritime nation whose short history had included the building of almost 2,500 ships for Atlantic commerce.

By comparison, the British had a large, well-organized navy with the following classes of ships: ships-of-the-line, 60 guns and over; frigates, 26 to 50 guns; sloops-of-war, 4 to 24 guns; brigs, about 20 guns; and naval schooners, 8 to 14 guns.

It was against elements of this gargantuan force that General George Washington moved when he recommended that all possible steps be taken to create a Continental Navy. On October 13, 1775, the birth of the Navy took place when Congress in Philadelphia decreed that two war vessels be

Ship-of-the-line.

Square-rigged frigate.

Sloop-of-War.

Brig-of-war under sail.

immediately fitted out to capture British shipping. Two more naval vessels were approved by the end of the month, at which time there had also been established an official Naval Committee, whose members were: John Adams, Silas Deane, John Langdon, Christopher Gadsden, Stephen Hopkins, Joseph Hewes, and R. H. Lee.

The first vessels commissioned in the new fleet were merchantmen made over into warships and named *Alfred, Columbus, Andrew Doria,* and *Cabot.* These were later joined by two schooners, *Wasp* and *Fly,* and the sloops *Providence* and *Hornet.* At the same time, approval was given to start construction in December, 1775, on thirteen regular warships.

On December 22, Esek Hopkins was appointed Commander in Chief of the first American naval fleet, and was given approval to lead the eight converted merchantmen to the Bahamas, where it was rumored there were vast stores of ammunition.

It was early in March, 1776, when he arrived and by a show of naval strength forced the governor of the islands into giving up his naval stores. The American fleet returned home with more than 85 artillery pieces and a great deal of valuable gunpowder.

Esek Hopkins then brought the little fleet into home waters and began a successful foray against enemy ships along the east coast. The *Columbus* under Captain Abraham Whipple, who had led the attack on the *Gaspée,* captured the British schooner *Hawk*

After the British armed cutter Margaretta *(left) had been grappled by the* Unity *(right), O'Brien's crew came over the rail with pitchforks and axes.*

on April 4, 1776. The *Alfred* overpowered the brig *Bolton* near Block Island, and two merchant vessels were seized. Then the fleet tangled with a 20-gun British ship, the *Glasgow*, in the same waters, and ran into difficulties. The *Cabot* was disabled and had four men killed and seven wounded; and both the *Alfred* and *Columbus* received additional casualties. The outcome was that the *Glasgow*, though badly damaged, made good her escape. Hopkins came under critical fire and several months later was dismissed as the only man ever to hold the title "Commander in Chief of the Fleet." Later naval judgment has been that the dismissal was a mistake, because Hopkins had strong qualities of initiative and leadership.

Eleven of the thirteen states had their own small navies for local defense against pirates along their own coasts. These were added to the Federal Navy upon its formation as supplementary forces rather than units of the fleet. Hence, the overall chain of command was somewhat confused at the start of the war.

Despite such problems, the growing American fleet was taking on British ships in individual engagements with considerable success. On April 17, 1776, the Continental brig *Lexington*, under Captain John Barry, captured the British sloop *Edward*. In May the American schooner *Wasp*, 8 guns, under Captain Charles Alexander, captured the English brig *Betsey*. During the same spring, Captain Nicholas Biddle was having considerable success in his ship, the *Andrew Doria*.

Off the New England coast he captured two British transports carrying troops, and brought in more than half a dozen other valuable prizes. Now, in naval circles, another name was being mentioned time after time—the name of John Paul Jones. In August, 1776, as captain of the *Providence,* he sailed north from Delaware and rounded up a total of sixteen enemy vessels as prizes of war, as well as destroying a number of others. Because of this record, he was given command of the *Alfred,* and sent out with the *Provi-* *dence* as support to ravage enemy shipping. In November he departed from Newport, and later captured the large British cargo ship *Mellish* and two other ships.

While Jones was prowling the ocean waters, a different kind of naval activity was taking place far inland, along the wild shores of Lake Champlain. General Benedict Arnold (not yet turned traitor to the American cause) had been fighting a losing battle with the British on land at Quebec in the winter of 1775-1776. Late in June he

retreated south along the shores of
Champlain, finally encamping at
Crown Point near the lower part of
the lake. A small American flotilla
had the run of the waters, having been
established there by Generals Philip
Schuyler, George Washington, and
Arnold himself.

The British, unable to advance south
without control of the lake, now began feverishly building war vessels to
try to wipe out the American fleet.
Not only would such a victory have
given the British control of Champlain, but it would have helped to cut
off the American forces in New England from those to the south.

Arnold, though remembered largely
as a commander of land forces, was in
fact an experienced seaman. He had
commanded merchant vessels before
the war, and had been a strong cham-
pion of American naval strength. Early
in October, word was received that the

15

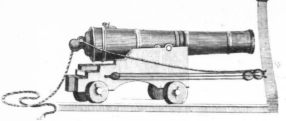

In Revolutionary times, cast-iron naval guns, like this one, were usually mounted on black-painted, wheeled truck carriages made of elm.

The plan of the hull of this American sloop-of-war (below) locates a bread locker (3); a coal locker (4); barrels of water (6); casks of rum (11); a shot locker (9); a shell room (10); and a powder magazine (15). Remaining areas were used for stowing gear and tackle.

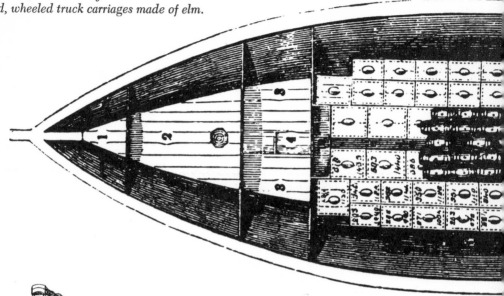

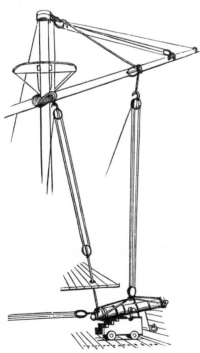

A gun is hoisted aboard an American ship by block-and-tackle secured to the main yardarm.

British had completed their furious shipbuilding program and were advancing south. They had twenty-five ships of assorted sizes, including the flagship *Inflexible*, with eighteen twelve-pounders, under the fleet commander, Commodore Thomas Pringle.

Out to meet this armada went the pitifully small American force: one small sloop, three light schooners, eight flat-bottomed gunboats (little more than barges with sails), and four small galleys. Armament consisted of 94 guns, largely ineffectual, and many of the 700 men had little or no naval experience. Arnold tried a clever stratagem. He moved his boats half

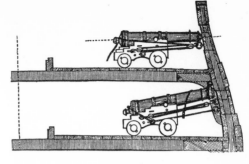

Naval guns of the Revolutionary period, shown on this page, were classified as 12-pounders, 24-pounders, or 32-pounders, according to the weight of the shot they fired. Range of the 18- and 24-pounders generally used on frigates was often well over a mile.

During a gale, cannon were securely lashed down. A loose gun, rolling back and forth, might kill men and seriously damage a ship.

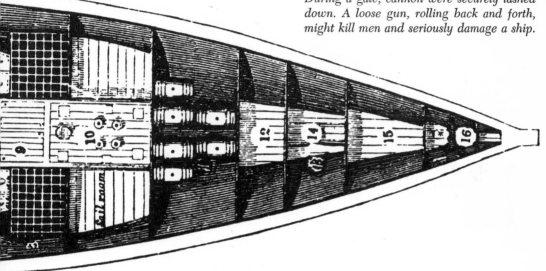

way up the lake to Valcour Island, on the west shore, and anchored in hiding until the British fleet had sailed past him before making his presence known. The British had to complete the awkward maneuver of coming about and attacking from leeward (the side of the boat *away* from the wind; the side of the boat *toward* the wind is called the windward side).

Arnold inflicted some damage, but the battle was far too one-sided. The schooner *Royal Savage* was so badly shot up she had to run ashore. The *New York* lost all her officers except her captain. The *Philadelphia* was so filled with holes she soon sank. And

the *Washington* was severely crippled. The Americans had by this time expended three-fourths of their meager supply of ammunition. So Arnold wisely ordered retreat south.

The escape was successful for the time being. Then, on October 12, the British started in pursuit. The *Washington,* having fallen far behind, was quickly captured by the *Inflexible* and

OVERLEAF: *In the North Sea, on September 23, 1779, John Paul Jones, aboard the* Bonhomme Richard, *fought his famous battle with the British ship* Serapis. *In the foreground, from left to right, are the* Serapis, *the* Richard *and the* Alliance. *At far right are the* Vengeance, *the* Pallas *and the* Scarborough.

17

Gustavus Conyngham   Nicholas Biddle

a 14-gun schooner, the *Maria*. The *Congress* was the next target for the British. Arnold and his men kept up a running two-hour battle, by which time the ship was all but demolished by enemy fire. Arnold then ran her ashore, set her afire along with four of the flat-bottomed gunboats, and escaped with his men into the woods.

The first battle of Lake Champlain was a decided naval victory for the British. But for the Americans it was, at least, a strategic victory. By the time the battle was over—on October 13—it was too late in the season for the British forces to advance, and they had to withdraw to Canada.

At sea, individual ships of the American Navy were astonishing the old-line British officers and seamen who had thought of the colonists as ill-trained and poorly equipped. During late 1776 and early 1777, Captain Lambert Wickes was annoying the British by capturing vessels in the enemy's own waters. One of the greatest surprises of all was in store for the captain

of an English ship, the *Prince of Orange*. Leisurely taking breakfast on May 3, 1777, in his private cabin, while his ship was cruising right in the middle of the English Channel, he looked up indignantly when a stranger burst in—an American officer.

"Sir," said the officer, one Gustavus Conyngham, "you will pardon me, but I am taking over your ship."

When the British officer stomped out on deck to reprimand his officers for permitting this intrusion, he was struck dumb with astonishment. For an American ship, the 10-gun *Surprise*, had lived up to her name by coming alongside in the heart of enemy waters and overpowering the British ship without firing a shot.

One of the finest American ships of the period was the frigate *Randolph*, 32 guns, commanded by Commodore Nicholas Biddle. On February 12, 1778, Biddle put out of Charleston with four vessels of the South Carolina navy: *General Moultrie*, 18; *Notre Dame*, 16; *Polly*, 16; and *Fair American*, 14. (In each instance the numeral denotes the number of guns carried.)

Heading into the West Indies, Biddle encountered a formidable enemy off Barbados, the strong, 64-gun ship-of-war *Yarmouth*. Not hesitating at being out-gunned two to one, Biddle lunged to the attack in the trim little *Randolph*. Almost at the start of the battle, Biddle was wounded badly. None of the other American ships had sufficiently heavy artillery to get into the battle, except for the *Moultrie*, which became confused and fired into the *Randolph* by mistake. For fifteen minutes the gallant Biddle raked the enemy back and forth, inflicting heavy damage, and suffering little hurt to his own ship. But in the moment of glory, as Biddle was waiting to get on the badly battered *Yarmouth's* quarter, the *Randolph* blew up.

Of the valiant crew of 315 officers and men, only four survived. Commodore Biddle was one of the casualties.

As the war progressed, the British found themselves more and more on the defensive. Those blasted Americans were not only sinking His Majesty's ships right and left, but had the audacity to attack right in the British home waters! On April 22, 1778, Captain John Paul Jones boldly sailed his ship, the *Ranger*, right into the harbor at Whitehaven, England, and set fire to the assembled shipping. He then landed his men, seized the battlements, and spiked the guns (drove iron spikes into the holes where the fuses were placed for setting off the cannon) so they would no longer fire.

In the fall of that year, with the *Ranger* turned over to a new commander, Jones went to France to bargain for a large vessel to add to the American fleet, an old Indiaman, the *Duc de Duras*. But what a vessel! She was about twelve years old, condemned because the rot had penetrated her planks.

Jones took her over forthwith.

"We will name you the *Bonhomme Richard*," said Jones, in honor of his friend, Benjamin Franklin, the author of *Poor Richard's Almanac*. *Bonhomme Richard* was the French translation of "Poor Richard". When it was translated, Franklin's *Poor Richard's Almanac* became enormously popular in France where its author was already much loved and admired. *Bonhomme Richard* became the kindly nickname the French gave Franklin himself.

The great, converted hulk put out of L'Orient on August 9, 1779. With her went the American ship *Alliance*, 36 guns; *Pallas*, 32; *Cerf*, 18; and *Vengeance*, 12. The French had entered the war partly because it was a good opportunity to attack an old enemy, Great Britain, and partly to share in the prizes captured.

Early in the afternoon of September 23, off Flamborough Head on the east coast of England, Jones sighted a large fleet of British merchant ships, escorted by the *Countess of Scarborough*, 20 guns, and by H. M. S. *Serapis*, a brand-

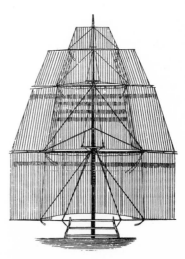

Frigate running before the wind.

An idealized print of Commodore Esek Hopkins (above) pictures the hero flanked by the Revolution's Rattlesnake and Pine Tree flags.

new frigate of 44 guns, under Captain Richard Pearson. Jones ordered his ships to the attack. The *Vengeance* went after the merchant ships, one at a time. The *Pallas* engaged the *Scarborough.* And Jones went straight for the *Serapis,* well aware that he was badly outgunned.

Both ships fired a broadside. On the *Bonhomme Richard,* this was disastrous. Two of her old 18-pounders promptly exploded, killing the gun crews and blowing out the deck above. Now the deadly new guns of the *Serapis* raked the rotten hull of the American ship from stem to stern, killing entire gun crews and putting the guns out of action one by one.

With his guns useless and the ship threatening to sink beneath him, the only hope Jones had was to engage in hand-to-hand battle. But his ship was clumsier than the Britisher. He had to try a trick. As the *Serapis* started to come about to rake the *Richard* with another broadside, Jones foxily filled his sails as though to try to escape. Then he abruptly turned into the wind, luffed, and caught his opponent off guard. The two ships came together with a mighty crash, bow to stern, stern to bow.

"Heave grapnels!" shouted Jones, and within seconds the ships were firmly locked.

At the last moment, Pearson, seeing

At left, John Paul Jones shoots an American sailor about to lower the Bonhomme Richard's *flag in surrender. It is probable that the story of the shooting is nothing but legend.*

what was happening, ordered his gunners to discharge their guns, and the gun deck of the *Bonhomme Richard* was literally ripped apart by the blast. Lieutenant Dale's few surviving gunners scrambled topside to fight with hand weapons. It was at this moment that one of the gunners, seeing the slaughter on deck, cried out "Quarter! Quarter!" This was the accepted cry of defeat.

"Have you struck?" shouted the British captain, hearing the cry.

"No!" replied John Paul Jones in words that have echoed down through history, "I have just begun to fight!"

Now it was the skill of the American seamen aloft—fighting from the ropes and platforms in the rigging—that was to play a large part in the battle. Marines and sailors, armed with muskets and hand grenades, cleared the British from the rigging of the *Serapis*, and then dropped hand grenades on the enemy and picked them off with musket fire. By 9:00 P.M. the leaking, blazing *Bonhomme Richard* was strewn with dead.

For a moment, it seemed that the British would rally. Jones held his ground, and the hand-to-hand fighting continued even more furiously. At 10:30, after three and a half hours of bloody battle, Captain Pearson struck his colors and the fight was over.

Two factors had brought about an American victory: sheer courage and grim determination. So badly wrecked was the *Bonhomme Richard* that she sank, and Jones took over the *Serapis* as his flagship. The cost of victory had been high: about half of the crew lost. But it was this action, more than any other in the Revolution, which established the American Navy as a fighting force of the very first order.

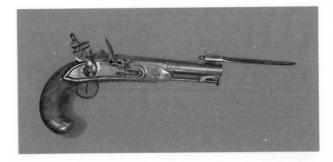

Captain Joshua Barney of the Continental Navy owned the boarding pistol shown at right. The 18th-century blunderbuss (below) is typical of the weapons used in repelling boarders on naval vessels in the colonial period.

From Yorktown to the Undeclared War with France

"The Navy must have the casting vote."

These words were written, not by a naval officer, but by General George Washington. As the American Army grew in strength and was able to trade the British redcoats blow for blow, Washington knew that victory would come only when he was able to engage in major battle and have the full support of a co-ordinated naval action behind him. He had reached this conclusion in 1778. Knowing that the Continental Congress could not supply him with the fleet he needed, he asked them to request naval support from the King of France. In the spring of 1781, Washington finally got his way. The French sent Admiral Comte de Grasse to North America. By late August, de Grasse had twenty-four ships-of-the-line in position near the entrance to Chesapeake Bay.

Then, on September 5, 1781, off Cape Henry, de Grasse's twenty-four vessels moved out of the bay to engage the nineteen ships-of-the-line of the British under Admiral Thomas Graves.

The battle, which lasted until September 9, was not decisive in a tactical sense. Yet it had far-reaching results, for Graves was forced to withdraw north to New York, and before the British Navy was able to redeploy a fleet for another attack, Washington had begun the famous siege of Yorktown on October 6, 1781. It was all over in two weeks. Cornwallis had nothing to do but surrender.

But it was not until more than a year later that a preliminary peace agreement was signed in Paris. And not until 1783 was the treaty officially agreed upon. In the meantime, American and British ships far at sea continued to battle wherever they met.

One of the last of these actions occurred on April 8, 1782. A converted merchantman named the *Hyder Ally*, 16, under the command of Joshua Barney, was convoying thirteen cargo vessels down the Delaware River.

As the convoy reached Cape May, three British warships were sighted, the largest being the *General Monk*, whose 18 guns carried twice the fire

In 1781, a French fleet (left) under Admiral de Grasse held the entrance to Chesapeake Bay and prevented the British fleet (right) of Admiral Graves from aiding General Cornwallis, whom Washington had trapped at Yorktown, Virginia.

After the Revolution, the ships of the Continental Navy were sold off, and by 1785 America owned no men-of-war. In 1793, England, Spain, and especially France began molesting American shipping. French privateers cruised the coasts, capturing merchant vessels of the United States. Seizures continued, causing President John Adams (right) to ask Congress to create the Department of the Navy on April 30, 1798. On May 18 of that year, Adams appointed Benjamin Stoddert (left) the first Secretary of the Navy. When Stoddert took office the Navy consisted of little more than three frigates. Three years later, when he retired, there were more than fifty ships in the fleet and six thousand men in service.

power of the *Hyder Ally*. Captain Barney was not the least dismayed. He ordered the merchant ships to retreat, and then lunged directly for the largest British ship, bypassing the two smaller British ships before they opened fire.

Barney knew he would be lost unless he could immediately "lock horns" with the enemy, rather than stand off and take heavy broadsides. So he tried a clever ruse. "When I shout my next order," he instructed the helmsman, "do just the *reverse*." He then shouted, "Hard a-port," loudly enough for the British to hear, and the helmsman swung to *starboard*. In this manner he suddenly brought the two ships together, but with his own in such a position that he could rake the enemy without getting much return fire.

Within seconds, his riflemen were picking off the British seamen aloft, and preparing to board. And, although the Americans were outgunned and outnumbered, Barney soon had the British striking their colors.

There was to be a long, barren period, however, in United States naval history right after the American Revolution. With some of her war vessels sold, and others rotting at wharves, the Navy degenerated to a point where,

Joshua Barney's frigate, the Hyder Ally *(left center), fires a broadside at the British warship* General Monk *during the battle in Delaware Bay.*

only ten years after Barney's battle, United States merchantmen were becoming easy prey to pirates and privateers from many countries. By 1785, the Continental Navy had ceased to exist. And in that year, an ominous incident occurred when an American merchantman, the *Maria*, was captured by Algerian pirates and her crew thrown into prison.

Not until 1794 did American anger force action. Congress, on March 27, authorized the building of six frigates, four of 44 guns each, the other two of 36. This was the *real beginning* of the U.S. Navy, with ships designed for but one purpose—fighting. The first of the six, the *United States*, was launched in May, 1797. The *Constellation* and *Constitution* followed shortly thereafter.

By this time, however, America had become involved in an undeclared war with France. For, eight years after de Grasse helped America win the battle of Yorktown, the French Revolution began. In 1792 France became a republic, and in 1793 King Louis XVI was executed. The French Republic had hoped for strong American support, but America proved to be unwilling to enter into close diplomatic and trade relations.

France was now openly at war with Great Britain, as England wanted to overthrow the French Republic. When the United States continued to trade with England, the French accused the Americans of carrying on trade hostile to France, and allowed their privateers to attack American ships.

Captain Joshua Barney

The first ship of the new Navy to see action was not one of the new frigates, but a converted merchantman, the *Delaware*. Under Captain Stephen Decatur (Senior), the 20-gun ship captured a French privateer, the *Croyable*, 14, off New Jersey on July 7, 1798. In November of that year, the American Navy received a hard blow when the *Baltimore*, returning from convoy duty near Havana, was set upon by two frigates, not French, but British. Despite the fact that the United States and Britain were now both fighting a common enemy, France, the British took off 55 members of the *Baltimore*'s crew and impressed them into service. This was the first major incident that was later to lead to the War of 1812.

Since most of the French privateers were operating out of the West Indies, the U.S. Navy concentrated its naval force in these waters, divided into four groups with a total of 21 frigates, brigs, sloops, and schooners. Commodores

Thomas Truxtun's Constellation *(right) capturing the French frigate* Insurgente *off the Caribbean island of Nevis, February 9, 1799.*

John Barry, commanding the *United States*, and Thomas Truxtun, commanding the *Constellation*, were particularly successful in defending American commerce in the Caribbean.

One of the finest American ships was the new frigate *Constellation* with 36 guns. On February 9, 1799, while cruising off the island of Nevis in the West Indies, she sighted the French frigate, the *Insurgente*, and gave immediate chase. Thomas Truxtun, the American commander, soon came within range, where he fired a broadside so effectively that it half demolished the *Insurgente's* quarterdeck. The French captain, Barreaut, seeing that the new guns of the American ship were stronger than his, tried vainly to close with the *Constellation* and take advantage of the fact that he had 100 more men than Truxtun. Time

Commodore Thomas Truxtun,
of the frigate Constellation

Commodore John Barry,
of the frigate United States

after time Truxtun passed directly across the bows of the enemy, where she could not return his fire, and raked her with broadsides. Within less than an hour after the battle started, the *Insurgente* struck her colors. She suffered seventy casualties, compared with one dead and two wounded on the *Constellation*.

During 1799, the United States Navy captured or sank almost thirty French privateers, but this did not stop the enemy from continuing to attack American merchant ships, until one important battle made the French take a different viewpoint. West of Guadeloupe, on February 1, 1800, Captain Truxtun sighted the French *Vengeance,* 52 guns. By eight that evening, he had come within hailing distance and called to the enemy to surrender.

The answer was a round of fire from the *Vengeance's* stern and quarter guns, directed at the American ship.

29

"Don't throw away a single shot," Truxtun ordered his gunners. "Fire directly into the hull of the enemy."

Truxtun had an enormous disadvantage to overcome. Knowing that the *Vengeance* had something like forty per cent greater firepower broadside to broadside, he took up a position on the enemy's windward side, where he could escape some of the guns. Now began one of the longest, bitterest battles in the history of sailing ships. From 8:00 that evening until 1:00 A.M. February 2, the ships viciously traded round for round. Truxtun had counted heavily on one vital factor: the skill of his gunners. He had seen this clearly demonstrated against the *Insurgente,* and he knew he could win if he could maintain absolute discipline in the ranks. By midnight the *Vengeance* had most of her guns out of action, and by

1:00 A.M. she was not able to fire at all.

Down came the enemy's colors, and Truxtun ordered the *Constellation* alongside to take his prize. But, even as he did so, he suffered a bitter setback. The *Vengeance* suddenly seemed to take new life. "She's sheering off, sir," reported one of the American officers. And so it was. The French frigate still had enough sail to get under way and slip off into the darkness.

By the end of the year 1799, the French had begun to feel that the undeclared war against the United States was a mistake. And after the embarrassing defeat of the *Vengeance*, one of their finest ships, by a smaller adversary, they were convinced of it. In March, 1800, an American peace mission was sent to Paris and by early fall a satisfactory agreement had been decided on by both nations.

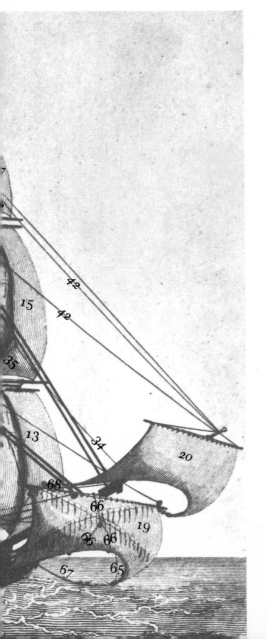

EXPLANATION OF THE REFERENCES ON THE PLATE
DELINEATING THE SQUARE SAILS OF A TWENTY GUN SHIP.

1	Fore courfe.	35	Fore topfail bowline bridles.
2	Main courfe.	36	Main topfail buntlines.
3	Fore topfail.	37	———— bowlines.
4	Main topfail.	38	———— bowline bridles.
5	Mizen topfail.	39	Mizen topfail buntlines.
6	Fore topgallant fail.	40	———— bowline.
7	Main topgallant fail.	41	———— bowline bridles.
8	Mizen topgallant fail.	42	Fore topgallant bowlines.
9	Fore royal.	43	———— bowline bridles.
10	Main royal.	44	Main topgallant bowlines.
11	Mizen royal.	45	———— bowline bridles.
12	Driver.	46	Mizen topgallant bowline.
13	Fore ftudding fails.	47	Fore royal haliards.
14	Main ftudding fails.	48	Main royal haliards.
15	Fore topmaft ftudding fails.	49	Mizen royal haliards.
16	Main topmaft ftudding fails.	50	Driver haliards.
17	Fore topgallant ftudding fails.	51	——— fheet.
18	Main topgallant ftudding fails.	52	——— down hauler.
19	Spritfail courfe.	53	Fore ftudding fail inner haliards.
20	Spritfail topfail.	54	Main ftudding fail inner haliards.
21	Fore fail fheets.	55	Fore ftudding fail boom guy.
22	——— tacks.	56	———————— tacks.
23	——— leech lines.	57	———————— fheets.
24	——— buntlines.	58	Main ftudding fail tacks.
25	——— bowlines.	59	Fore topmaft ftudding fail down hauler.
26	——— bowline bridles.	60	———————— tack.
27	Main fheets.	61	Main topmaft ftudding fail downhauler.
28	——— tack.	62	———————— tack.
29	Mailfail leech lines.	63	Fore topgallant ftudding fail tack.
30	——— buntlines.	64	Main topgallant ftudding fail tack.
31	——— bowlines.	65	Spritfail clue line.
32	——— bowline bridles.	66	———— buntline.
33	Fore topfail buntlines.	67	———— fheets.
34	———— bowlines.	68	———— topfail fheets.

This sail plan of a square-rigged, twenty-gun ship appeared in 1789 in a manual used by the American Navy. The book was entitled The Elements and Practice of Rigging and Seamanship.

The Brave Tars of America granting Peace to the Barbary States.

The Gallant Decatur and his Brave Tars Capturing the Algerine Admiral.

The Barbary Pirates

"Port your helm! Port your helm!"

The orders of Captain William Bainbridge rang out on the deck of the trim new frigate *Philadelphia*, 36 guns, as she moved into the harbor of Tripoli on October 31, 1803. But it was already too late; the trim hull shuddered underfoot as the keel grated against uncharted rocks.

Now officers and crew moved swiftly, trying desperately to fill the sails again and heel the ship still farther so she might slip loose. It was no use. Bainbridge ordered all surplus cargo dumped overboard.

Why was he so desperate in his attempts to lighten the vessel immediately? Part of the answer lay in the warning cry from the lookout, "Here they come!" as Tripolitan gunboats were sighted putting out from under

An American naval officer's gold sword belt buckle (top), decorated with eagles and entwined serpents, dates from around 1800. The dirk with ivory handle and gold scabbard was presented by Act of Congress to Midshipman Edward Trenchard in recognition of his services during the action at Tripoli in 1804.

the shadows of the great fort. And part lay in the reasons for the *Philadelphia* having been there in the first place. For since the spring of 1801, the United States had been engaged in war—this time completely a naval one—with the Barbary nation, Tripoli.

The spark that set off the conflict had actually occurred, as mentioned earlier, with the capture of the American schooner *Maria* by Algerine pirates in July, 1785. During the next fifteen years there were numerous such incidents, leading to a type of extortion

piece of early 19th-century chintz (left) is printed with a repeating pattern.
center panel, flanked by portraits of Bainbridge and Decatur, shows the "Brave
s of America Granting Peace to the Barbary States" in 1805. Panels at top and
om picture Decatur capturing an Algerian frigate in the "Algerine War" of 1815.

by the Barbary nations (Morocco, Algiers, Tunis, and Tripoli) in which they exacted tribute from the United States in return for refraining from attacking American ships in the Mediterranean. In 1796, the United States permitted the shameful approval of tribute money in the amount of $56,000 to be paid the powerful Pasha (ruler) of Tripoli for this purpose, and an even larger sum was paid to Algiers as similar extortion money. The aging George Washington strongly opposed such conduct.

By 1801, the American leaders were very angry about the situation. When the government refused to consent to new demands, the Pasha of Tripoli finally declared open war on the United States as of May 10. By July, the United States Navy had dispatched a squadron under Commodore Richard Dale to Gibraltar. The flagship was the frigate *President,* 44, along with the *Philadelphia,* 36, the *Essex,* 32, and a 12-gun schooner, the *Enterprise.*

In March, 1802, after little action, the squadron was disbanded and a stronger one organized to supplement it: the *Constellation,* 36; *Chesapeake,* 36; *Adams,* 28; *New York,* 36; and *John Adams,* 28. In 1803, Commodore Edward Preble arrived in the staunch American frigate *Constitution,* 44 guns, with a number of other vessels.

Now things began to happen. Preble had purposely brought along small ships like the 12-gun *Vixen* and the 16-gun *Argus*—the latter under the command of one Lieutenant Stephen Decatur, Jr. (son of Captain Decatur of the *Delaware*).

With these smaller ships, Preble in-

stituted a series of raids against the Barbary powers and was ready to concentrate his strength against the worst of these opponents: Tripoli. In late October, 1803, the frigate *Philadelphia*, under the command of Captain William Bainbridge, was dispatched to blockade the port. And it was at this time that the *Philadelphia*, as we have already seen, ran aground while chasing an enemy vessel too close to shore.

As Captain Bainbridge and his crew tried desperately to free the frigate from the shoals, the enemy could be seen approaching in great numbers in the small Tripolitan gunboats. Every-

35

On the night of February 16, 1804, Lieutenant Stephen Decatur and 84 volunteers aboard the ketch Intrepid (above, left) sailed into the harbor at Tripoli and burned the captured frigate Philadelphia. England's Lord Nelson, the hero of Trafalgar, called Decatur's deed the most daring act of the age. Six months later Captain Richard Somers loaded the Intrepid with gunpowder and sailed into the harbor, determined to destroy the Tripolitan fleet. Before he could accomplish his mission, the Tripolines sighted the Intrepid, opened fire, and blew her up (below), killing Somers and his entire crew.

thing possible was tried—pumping the bilges dry, heaving the forward guns overboard, chopping down the foremast. None of these emergency moves helped. The cautious enemy gunboats approached so that the way in which the *Philadelphia* listed (tilted to one side) was in their favor and the American guns could not be brought to bear. Bainbridge was forced to surrender, with 22 officers and 315 men, and the enemy eventually worked the *Philadelphia* free at flood tide and towed her into a deeper part of the harbor.

Now Commodore Preble had a new and worrisome problem on his hands. Not only had he lost one of his finest ships and several hundred men, but once the enemy had trained a proper crew, it would use the *Philadelphia* against the Americans. Preble worked out a daring plan, and for it selected one of his ablest young officers, Lieutenant Stephen Decatur, Jr.

Earlier in the war, an ancient 60-ton ketch, the *Mastico*, had been captured from the Tripolitans. Decatur was to sail her, as a "trader," directly into the harbor at Tripoli. The pilot would be a Maltese seaman named Catalano, and on deck would be a number of Americans dressed in Maltese clothing. Below decks, however, would be seventy-five other Americans, with a supply of combustibles for setting fire to the *Philadelphia*.

Decatur hand-picked eighty-four volunteers, and the first week in February, 1804, found the little vessel, now renamed the *Intrepid,* heading for Tripoli. Now trouble began. The little vessel was struck by a heavy storm. Food and water began running low. The men were constantly seasick. Since they had no change of clothing, they were constantly wet and miserable. Yet, somehow, by February 16, they managed to reach the harbor entrance, still afloat. Then a new problem arose.

According to plan, some boats from the 16-gun American brig, *Siren,* which lay three miles out to sea, were to move in under cover of darkness and assist the *Intrepid's* men to escape after they had fired the *Philadelphia*. But, following the storm, a calm settled on the ocean, and the *Siren's* boats could not make the rendezvous in time. Decatur waited as long as he could, then gave orders to proceed.

One hundred yards from the *Philadelphia,* the *Intrepid* was hailed and ordered to anchor where she stood. But Decatur was ready with a ruse that was part of the plan. "Tell them," he instructed the Maltese pilot, "that we lost our anchors in the storm and would like to tie alongside, just overnight."

The ruse worked. Within a few minutes, Catalano had rowed over to the *Philadelphia* with a line, and several sleepy looking Tripolitan seamen were actually aiding the American cause by pulling the *Intrepid* in close. As the ships closed, Decatur gave the signal. Up leaped the Americans, pouring out of the *Intrepid's* cramped hold.

"*Americanos!*" shouted a pirate on

watch on the *Philadelphia's* deck. As cries echoed through the ship, enemy seamen scrambled topside, many so terrified that they dove overboard. Now the Americans were slashing away with cutlasses, firing pistols, and creating such havoc that within a few minutes twenty of the enemy lay dead and resistance was over.

"Strike out the combustibles!" ordered Decatur. From the deck of the *Intrepid*, pound after pound of powder and matches were tossed upward. And within twenty minutes the *Philadelphia* was a raging inferno. Now the guns of the fort at Tripoli were coming into action, sending round upon round wildly across the bay. But the *Intrepid* was already escaping, making her way to the harbor entrance before the Tripolitans could muster their

gunboats and give chase.

The outcome of this incident, one that covered the name of Lieutenant Stephen Decatur with great glory, was that the Pasha of Tripoli was furious. In his great anger, he demanded that the Americans *pay him* for the loss of the *Philadelphia,* in the sum of half a million dollars! Upon hearing this audacious demand, Commodore Preble laughed outright and asserted that force, not tribute, was the key to making the Barbary nations more respectful of the American flag.

Consequently, he set sail on July 14 of that year, 1804, from Syracuse with the *Constitution,* the *Nautilus,* the *Enterprise,* six gunboats, and two mortarboats. His objective: to attack Tripoli's shipping and fortifications and so harass the Pasha that he would be re-

ceptive to peace terms. During a five-week period in August and part of September he completed five separate attacks with considerable success. Rather than scatter his shots, by attacking the other Barbary powers (Algiers, Tunis, and Morocco), he wisely surmised that a victory against Tripoli would in turn lead the other enemy nations to accept American terms.

The strange naval war against Tripoli, while often mentioned as a "little war," was actually of far more importance to American history than its size and scope would indicate. It taught the United States that a great nation could not exist without a great navy and that an honorable peace could never be purchased. And it served as one of the finest training grounds ever for the fledgling American Navy.

The Pasha soon came to realize, through Preble's constant and continuing attacks, that further conflict could only be disastrous for him. Still, he refused to end the war. The Americans postponed further operations until spring.

On April 27, 1805, the Tripolitan port of Derna was attacked by several hundred Arabs on land under the command of Hamet Karamanli, ex-Pasha of Tripoli, who wanted to become Pasha again. Karamanli was largely successful because of the assistance of an American civilian, Mr. William Eaton, a consular agent, and Lieuten-

This painting shows Commodore Preble's ships bombarding the fort at Tripoli on August 3, 1804. The towering Constitution *is flanked by gunboats at left and mortar boats at right. At rear are the Pasha's lateen-rigged ships.*

ant O'Bannon, with Midshipman Peck and seven marines from the brig *Argus*. Seeing an opportunity to improve his position, Preble had dispatched the *Argus, Hornet,* and *Nautilus* to launch a co-ordinated attack from the sea at the same time. Derna was quickly captured, and held until after the Pasha had finally agreed to peace negotiations. The war against Tripoli officially came to an end with the signing of the peace treaty on June 10, 1805.

Peace with Tripoli, however, did not completely end America's troubles with the Barbary powers. As early as 1807, the Dey (or ruler) of Algiers again began capturing American ships and enslaving their crews and passengers. The War of 1812 prevented the United States from taking strong action against Algiers, but on March 2, 1815, eight days after peace had been signed with England, Congress declared war. The "Algerine War," as it was sometimes called, lasted a year and ended when the Dey was forced to sign a peace treaty in 1816, after many defeats suffered by his fleet at the hands of two powerful American naval squadrons commanded by Commodores Decatur and Bainbridge. America's troubles with the Barbary powers were finally at an end.

The heroes of Tripoli were Stephen Decatur (above) and Commodore Edward Preble (below). Decatur, made commodore in 1813, once toasted the nation, saying, "May she always be in the right; but our country, right or wrong."

On June 1, 1813, off Boston, the American frigate Chesapeake *was captured by the British ship* Shannon. *The picture above shows Captain Philip Broke, sword in hand, boarding the American vessel. As wounded Captain James Lawrence of the* Chesapeake *lay dying, he uttered one of the most famous battle cries of the war: "Don't give up the ship!" The picture below shows the British* Java *exploding off the coast of Brazil on December 29, 1812. The* Java *had surrendered to Commodore Bainbridge's* Constitution *after a two-hour fight. She was so badly damaged that Bainbridge removed the English and fired the hulk.*

The Naval War of 1812

The U.S. frigate *Chesapeake* was a trim vessel, well armed with 36 strong guns. But she was at a distinct disadvantage that June day in 1807 when approached by the large British frigate *Leopard* near Cape Henry. It was not simply because the *Leopard* had 50 guns, but because this was a time of peace between the two nations and Captain James Barron of the *Chesapeake* was expecting no trouble.

"I am sending a boarding party over," shouted the British captain.

"For what purpose?" asked the astonished Barron.

"You have British seamen aboard who have illegally deserted."

That, said Captain James Barron, was a diplomatic matter to be determined through proper channels. By way of answer, the British commander fired a broadside which killed or wounded twenty-one men. With the American ship thus forced into submission, the English boarded her and forcibly removed four seamen, one of whom had deserted from a British

ship, but the other three being rightful American citizens.

It was this type of incident that helped bring about the War of 1812. During the next five years, the British not only continued to impress American seamen on the high seas, but they also blockaded American ports.

On May 16, 1811, the first action began when the American frigate *President,* under Commodore John Rodgers, exchanged shots with the British sloop-of-war *Little Belt,* causing some thirty-two casualties on the latter before both ships withdrew in the night. But the war officially began on June 18, 1812, when American leaders could no longer tolerate the British disregard of America's position as an independent nation. Statistically, it was completely foolhardy for the United States to declare war on a nation as powerful as Great Britain. The

U.S. Navy had sixteen warships, the finest of them being the 44-gun frigates *Constitution, United States,* and *President;* the 36-gun frigates *Chesapeake, Congress,* and *Constellation;* and the 32-gun *Essex.* In contrast to this, the mighty British Navy possessed some 600 warships, including 124 ships-of-the-line and 116 frigates.

Shortly after the outbreak of hostilities, the British assigned the large ship-of-the-line *Africa,* 64 guns, and an escort of four fast frigates to head southward from Halifax to engage whatever American warships they encountered. Meanwhile, heading north from the Chesapeake, the American frigate *Constitution,* under Captain Isaac Hull, made for New York to protect American shipping there. Hull did not know it, but he was running directly into a trap.

Off the coast of New York, on July 17, the *Constitution* found herself becalmed, with enemy sails on all sides—

The Navy's first steam battleship, designed by Robert Fulton, was known as Demologos, *or* Fulton the First. *It guarded New York harbor but fought no battles during the War of 1812.*

those of the *Africa* and her escorts. But Hull, one of the finest seamen of his day, had a few tricks up his sleeve. He ordered his boats out to *tow* the *Constitution.* In this way, he gained considerable headway. And when the British tried the same maneuver, Hull countered with another one. He sent one boat far out in front, with small anchors and trailing a hawser astern. When the boat reached the limits of the hawser, the anchors were dropped.

"Man the anchor winch!" The cry rang out sharp and clear, and within minutes the *Constitution* was being pulled furiously forward in a process known as kedging. All that day of the seventeenth, the American frigate stayed out of range. Then, on the eighteenth, Hull proved what a superb seaman he was by wetting his sails to hold the breeze better, and outsailing the British. On the nineteenth, as the race continued, Hull executed one more trick to fool the enemy. Hit by a passing wind squall, he let the sails run loose to give the effect of utmost confusion. The British, seeing this, made great haste to furl and reef (or shorten) their own sails. Whereupon, the *Constitution* was brought immediately under trim and was well on her way to escape before the British could set full sail and get up headway again.

During the month of August, 1812, the British were to see even more of

the skill of the United States Navy. On the thirteenth, the American frigate *Essex,* commanded by Captain David Porter, captured the *Alert* after a brief battle, and within the next four weeks went on to take nine other prizes. And the *Constitution,* off the coast of Halifax, Nova Scotia, on August 19, sighted the powerful British frigate, *Guerrière,* 38, and gave chase. The latter was under the command of Captain Dacres, an able skipper, but one who had little respect for the American Navy. As the trim American ship bore down on him, he prepared for what he was certain would be an easy victory.

It was 5:00 P.M. when the *Guerrière*

prematurely opened fire. Captain Isaac Hull was not the slightest bit impressed. "Hold your fire," he told his gunnery officers, as the *Constitution* rode towards her opponent.

At 6:00 P.M., when the *Constitution* had sailed to within less than 100 yards of the *Guerrière,* and on her port beam, Hull finally gave the order to fire. With both ships running before the wind, in a southeasterly direction, Hull and Dacres exchanged broadside after broadside directly at each other. The British captain was certain that

OVERLEAF: *The victory of the frigate* Constitution *over the* Guerrière, *August 19, 1812.*

45

now his gunners would strike the American vessel with telling effect. Dacres was, however, astounded to see shot after shot striking the *Guerrière's* hull, sometimes making holes below the waterline, while the best his own gunners seemed able to do was rip through some of the *Constitution's* rigging. The American gunners now concentrated their fire on the masts of the British ship, and about twenty minutes after the battle had begun, succeeded in knocking down the mizzenmast. Then part of the *Guerrière's* mainmast was shot away. So close were the two ships at one point that all at once the enemy bowsprit became entangled in the rigging of the *Constitution* and a cry rang out.

"Boarders away!"

There followed a brief hand-to-hand battle. It was not to last long, for the *Guerrière* wrenched loose again and backed off. At the same time, the rest of her mainmast toppled and the foremast came down in a tangle of debris. The battle was over. The *Guerrière's* colors came down, and the stunned British captain, Dacres, surrendered. This battle has gone down in American history as one of the greatest of the entire war. Strategically, it was not of great importance. The British could afford to lose one frigate in battle. But for the Americans, this was a tremendous boost to morale.

On October 25, 1812, another famous battle took place, this time far across the Atlantic, some 600 miles west of the Canary Isles. The American frigate, *United States*, 44, under the able command of an officer already noted for his bravery and skill, Stephen Decatur, encountered the slightly smaller British frigate, *Macedonian*, 38. The battle lasted two and a half hours. In part, this was because Decatur deliberately avoided closing in for point-blank broadsides. He cut the enemy down bit by bit, so that when the British finally surrendered, he had a valuable prize to capture, and not (as in the case of the *Guerrière*) a shattered hulk.

In the meantime, the famous *Constitution* was continuing to make a name for herself. On December 29, 1812, while sailing off the coast of Brazil under Captain William Bainbridge, she encountered the British frigate *Java*, 44. Both vessels were nearly equal in size, firepower, and speed, and both had highly experienced officers and men. From 2:00 in the afternoon until 5:30 the battle proceeded.

The American ship was handicapped early in the fight when her wheel was shot away, and Bainbridge had to steer by using men at the rudder tackles two decks below where he stood giving orders. Nevertheless, Bainbridge never let the British gain the advantage. Though he himself was seriously wounded, he remained at his post. Around five o'clock, the two ships came together and boarding parties went at each other. At 5:30 the British gave up. The *Java* had a total of 124 men killed and wounded. And it was because the *Constitution's* hull had

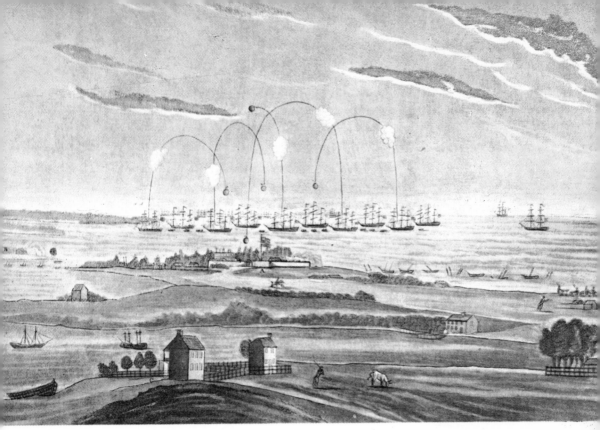

A British fleet bombed Fort McHenry in Baltimore during the night of September 13-14, 1814. Aboard one of these ships was an American prisoner, Francis Scott Key, who saw, in the light of "bombs bursting in air," that "our flag was still there." The thrilling sight inspired him to write the words of the national anthem, The Star-Spangled Banner.

resisted the British cannon balls so stoutly in this fight that she was nicknamed "Old Ironsides."

Despite notable victories in 1813 such as the one in which the *Hornet*, an 18-gun sloop-of-war, beat the British brig *Peacock*, 18, the American Navy also suffered tragic losses. One of the most notable came on June 1, 1813, as His Majesty's frigate, *Shannon*, 38, boldly patrolled the coast off the very mouth of Boston Harbor. Captain Broke of the *Shannon* learned that an American frigate, the *Chesapeake*, 36, lay in the harbor being refitted. He sent a written message challenging her to fight a ship-to-ship duel.

Long before the message was re-ceived, the *Chesapeake* had already put to sea to attack the marauder. In command was a new captain, thirty-two-year-old James Lawrence. His eagerness to take on the *Shannon* outweighed his judgment, for he had nothing to gain. He had an inexperienced crew, whereas Broke, who had been in command of his ship for seven years, had a tight, well-disciplined group of seamen. And the American frigate was badly needed on the high seas, where she could attack British merchant ships.

On June 1, Lawrence sailed resolutely out to meet the enemy. The two ships came within range at 5:50 in the afternoon. The *Chesapeake's* first mis-

Commodore
Oliver Hazard Perry

Commodore
Isaac Hull

Commodore
William Bainbridge

Captain
James Lawrence

Commodore
David Porter

Commodore
Thomas Macdonough

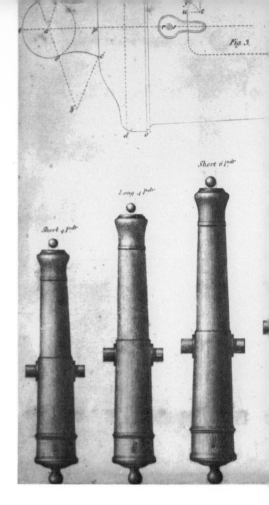

take was moving slightly ahead of the *Shannon* as the two vessels sailed southeast. The *Shannon* launched a broadside. The sailing master (who navigated the ship) was killed instantly, along with several other American officers. And Lawrence himself received a wound that was to be fatal.

During the confusion that followed, the *Chesapeake* swung partially into the wind, then drifted back again toward her opponent. As the two ships crashed together, the British swiftly boarded the *Chesapeake*.

American casualties were heavy: during the fighting, which lasted a total of only fifteen minutes, forty-eight men were killed and ninety-seven

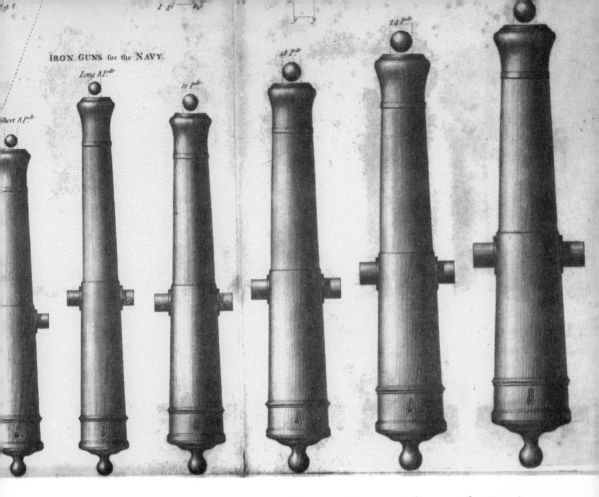

These naval cannon of the era of the War of 1812 range from 4- to 36-pounders. The 24-pounder was standard on American ships.

wounded. British losses were high too, forty-three killed and twenty-nine wounded, the latter group including Captain Broke, who received a bad pistol wound as his payment for challenging the Americans. Captain James Lawrence managed, even in defeat, to strike an unexpected blow at the British. As he lay dying, he rose up and ordered the officers who attended him, "Don't give up the ship!"

Little did those who attended the mortally wounded commander realize that here was a battle cry which—through circumstances they could not possibly foresee—would ring down through the pages of American history.

"Don't give up the ship!"

These were more than the resolute words of a dying man—this was the battle slogan that was to fly from the masthead of the 20-gun ship named after Lawrence during the most important single action of the War of 1812, the Battle of Lake Erie.

During the fall of 1812, a naval lieutenant, Jesse D. Elliott, had been sent to Lake Erie to strengthen America's position along a waterway vital to holding the vast territories to the west. He purchased several small vessels and established a naval base. Then, in the following winter, 150 seamen were

51

Commodore Perry's ships sail toward the English fleet (left) at the beginning of the Battle of Lake Erie, on September 10, 1813.

sent to Lake Erie, followed in March by the man who was to command them, Oliver Hazard Perry.

When the British heard about this American assignment, they were inclined to look down their noses at it. Not only was Perry young (at twenty-seven) for such a responsibility, but he was expected to accomplish the impossible. Many of the ships he was to command were still nothing but trees in the forest. And the artillery and ammunition would have to be transported hundreds of miles over rough roads and narrow streams to get to the naval base. The British made one tragic mistake when they violated a cardinal rule of warfare: "Never underestimate the power of the enemy."

Perry was a dynamo. He organized a furious shipbuilding program. He established fortifications and outposts and supplied them with local militia, to frustrate British attempts to capture his tiny shipyards.

By July, Perry had two brigs completed, the *Lawrence* and the *Niagara*. Each ship had eighteen "short 32's" and two "long 12's." In the meantime, the British, under the command of Barclay, were building a 19-gun warship, the *Detroit*, to add to the flotilla already in service: the *Queen Charlotte*, 17; *Lady Prevost*, 13; *Hunter*, 10; *Little Belt*, 3; *and Chippewa*, 1.

As dawn broke on September 10,

1813, the American force under Perry proceeded up the lake from Put-in-Bay; while from the north Barclay sailed down to meet him. The Americans approached from the windward side in the following order: the schooners *Scorpion* and *Ariel*, 4; the flagship *Lawrence*, 20; the brig *Caledonia*, 3; the brig *Niagara*, 20; and three poorly armed schooners, the *Somers*, 2; *Porcupine*, 1; and *Tigress*, 1; and the sloop *Trippe*, 1.

Around noon the two fleets came together. The 20-gun *Niagara*, which, with the *Lawrence*, was to carry the heaviest burden of battle, failed to

come up into position for almost two hours. This meant that the *Lawrence* alone bore the brunt of the initial clash. The flagships were heavily damaged and suffered many casualities. By 2:00 P.M., the *Lawrence* was completely out of action. She had eighty-three men killed and wounded. Captain Perry had fired his last serviceable gun, and capture would have been inevitable had not the *Niagara* finally arrived.

Now it was that Perry made his heroic stand. Risking death, he put out in an open boat for the *Niagara*, proudly displaying the battle pennant with the never-to-be-forgotten inscription,

"Don't Give Up The Ship."

Once aboard the *Niagara* Perry headed point-blank for the enemy. As he hit the British line, he opened fire with his port guns at the small British warships *Lady Prevost* and *Chippewa*, and at the same time with his starboard guns against the *Detroit* and *Charlotte*.

The enemy was unprepared for this bold move. The *Detroit* and *Charlotte* ran afoul of each other and were for a time dead in the water. Perry veered to starboard, to pass along the other side of the two ships and rake them with additional broadsides. At 3:00

53

This drawing shows a British sailor tied to a grating, about to receive a flogging. In the era of the War of 1812 this brutal discipline was common to the navies of the world, but was abolished in the United States in 1850.

P.M., the flag of the *Detroit* was hauled down. The other British ships surrendered in quick sucession.

In his report, Perry wrote: "We have met the enemy and they are ours . . ."

After that day, British strength in northwestern Ohio was on the wane. But this was not true all along the border. Just as American hopes looked brightest, the tides of fortune began to turn. In the spring of 1814, the British started massing troops in Canada, to move southward across Lake Champlain. They also began to assemble a fleet of sixteen ships.

All through the late spring and early summer, the Americans awaited the great invasion. As they did so, isolated duels were taking place at sea. In

April, the 22-gun American sloop *Frolic* surrendered to the much larger *Orpheus*, 36 guns, and the U.S.S. *Peacock* evened the score by beating the brig *Epervier*, both ships rated at 18 guns. In June, the American sloop-of-war *Wasp*, 22, captured a British ship of similar size, the *Reindeer*. And so the seesaw battles went.

But two months later, the entire country was to be shocked by the failure to organize an adequate defense of Washington and the subsequent capture and burning of the city by British troops. Commodore Joshua Barney, with a small force of 500 sailors and marines, made the only creditable showing, standing at Bladensburg until outflanked by the enemy and deserted

54

by the raw recruits who made up the American Army. Later on, Commodore Perry, along with John Rodgers and David Porter, made an attempt to halt the British along the Potomac. But they were finally forced to retreat.

After thus running rampant in the very heart of the American capital, the British began the movement south over Lake Champlain. Commodore George Downie, the British commander, had distinct naval superiority over the Americans. His squadron consisted of twelve gunboats; the brig *Linnet*, 16 guns; the sloops *Chubb* and *Finch*, each with 11 guns; and, heading the list, a full-size 37-gun frigate, the *Confiance*. By September, he was ready.

Opposing this force was an American squadron of ten gunboats, plus four ships: the flagship *Saratoga*, 26 guns; the brig *Eagle*, 20; the converted schooner *Ticonderoga*, 17; and a small sloop, the *Preble*, 7. Commanding this force was Captain Thomas Macdonough.

Macdonough knew that the British would make the attack and decided to begin the battle *with his ships at anchor*, rather than on the open lake. He selected a bay right off Plattsburgh, New York, then partially held by the British. Here, just out of range of the enemy shore batteries, he lined up his little squadron in a position facing east. At the northern end of the line, he stationed the *Eagle*. Supporting her were three gunboats. Then came the *Saratoga* and two gunboats; the *Ticonderoga* and two gunboats; and the

Clinging to a yardarm high above deck, these sailors unfurl the huge square-rigged sails.

A gun crew of 1812 train their heavy cannon by shifting it on the skids with handspikes.

No distance from their gunport, the crewmen slept in hammocks slung in the 'tweendecks.

55

The Battle of Lake Champlain, as this picture indicates, was a naval and a land fight. Macdonough's naval victory on September 11, 1814, caused the retreat of British land forces under General Prevost.

little *Preble* with three gunboats.

Macdonough reasoned correctly that the British fleet would have to attack directly from the east. He placed his four ships in a manner that would put them broadside to the approaching enemy. This meant that the British would be advancing against heavy fire from the start and that initially they would have a distinct disadvantage because they could return that fire only with a few of their forward guns, and not with any broadsides.

At 9:00 A.M. on September 11, 1814, the well-armed British flagship defiantly approached for an attack—far ahead of the other ships. Luck favored the Americans when the wind died down, and the British frigate not only lost speed, but also maneuverability. "Commence firing!" ordered Macdonough, and the *Confiance* now bore the full broadside blast of the four American warships. Nevertheless, her superior firepower was not by any means wasted. From 400 yards away, she brought her bow guns to bear on the *Eagle*, then swung slightly to give a raking broadside to the *Saratoga*, which killed or wounded nearly one-fifth of the latter's men.

At the north end of the line, the 11-gun *Chubb* also engaged the Americans, but the *Eagle*'s marksmanship and heavier guns quickly knocked the British ship out of action. The 16-gun

Linnet fared much better, first harassing the *Eagle* with highly effective fire, then inflicting some damage on the *Saratoga*. To the south, the *Finch*, 11, attacked the 17-gun converted American schooner *Ticonderoga*, but was badly damaged, went out of control, and drifted on the reefs at Crab Island.

By 11:00 A.M., the *Saratoga* was a pitiful sight. Macdonough had been wounded by flying fragments, yet he remained at his post. When the guns on one side of the ship were completely knocked out of action, and when the rigging was so badly shattered that the ship would not sail, he still had one trick left. He ordered his men to "wind

ship." The stern anchor was dropped, and the cable to the bow anchor cut, in such a way that wind and current would swing the ship 180 degrees around. This brought the few remaining guns on the *other* side to bear on the large *Confiance*.

The British flagship was in even worse condition. A little after 11:00 A.M., she surrendered, the valiant Captain Downie long since killed in action. The other British ships quickly followed suit. When casualties were counted, the Americans had 52 men killed and 59 wounded; the British 84 men killed and 110 wounded.

As soon as the defeat of Downie's squadron seemed inevitable, the British Army began to move out of Plattsburgh. Thus ended British invasion plans from the north, and with them much of Great Britain's enthusiasm for continuing the costly war. Few engagements of any importance occurred after the Battle of Lake Champlain. A treaty of peace was signed at Ghent the day before Christmas, 1814. Both sides gradually called in their far-flung ships, and hostilities slowly died out. The United States could no longer be thought of by England and other European countries as a rebellious group of upstart colonies. It had taken its place in the world as a power.

Join the Navy and
See the World

With the War of 1812 finally brought to an end, the United States entered an era of comparative peace, but one that was to be marked with some notable deeds by the United States Navy. On August 19, 1818, Captain James Biddle climaxed a long voyage in the American sloop *Ontario* by landing at Cape Disappointment, at the mouth of the Columbia River in the Pacific Northwest, and taking possession of the Oregon Territory for the United States.

And a year later, in August of 1819, Oliver Hazard Perry was to die in a different kind of battle from the ones for which he was so gloriously noted. After concluding a treaty with Venezuela, he contracted yellow fever while returning to his ship and became one of the Navy's most tragic peacetime casualties.

The fact that this was an era of peace did not mean that the Navy had no sea battles to fight. Throughout

The Navy was often called upon to protect American interests abroad. When some American sailors aboard a Salem pepper trader were killed in Quallah Battoo, Sumatra, the Navy dispatched the Potomac and landed marines (left) in Sumatra in February, 1832, to bolster the nation's prestige.

The sketch (below) by the Navy's Lieutenant Charles Wilkes, was made in the Antarctic in 1838. In 1829 and 1830, Wilkes sailed with the Vincennes, the first American naval vessel to sail around the world. From 1838 to 1842 he commanded the important naval expedition which explored the South Pacific, Antarctica, and the Pacific Northwest.

Probably more than ninety per cent of America's sailors of the nineteenth century wore tattoos such as those above. An anchor used to mean that a seaman had cruised the Atlantic; a full-rigged ship, that he had sailed 'round Cape Horn; and a dragon, that he had voyaged to China. The Chinese lacquered tray (below) shows the American, British, and Dutch "hongs" or trading wharves in Canton, China, in 1825, when more Yankee merchantmen traded with India and China than did the ships of any other country except England. In 1840, this rich commerce ceased during the "Opium War" between China and Britain; but Commodore Kearny reopened Canton to American trade in 1842, which action greatly aided the signing of an American trade treaty with the Chinese in 1844.

the Caribbean, a new breed of pirate was emerging—privateers helping the South American revolutionists in their battle against Spain, but who soon began attacking ships of other nationalities too when they found how easy prize money was to come by. The ten-year period starting around 1814 was the worst, and it was during this time that the American Navy organized the effective West India Squadron to deal with the problem. The Squadron actually did not start operations until 1822, at which time it was made up of two fast frigates, four sloops, four schooners, two brigs, and a pair of gunboats. A year later eight new schooners were added, along with the first naval steamboat to see action in battle: a converted ferryboat.

Another Navy duty was the suppression of the African slave trade, flourishing right after the War of 1812. In 1819, Congress passed an act giving the Navy power to capture slave ships, and early in 1820, the American sloop-of-war *Cyane* began cruising the coast of Africa and proved to be a great factor in stamping out this inhuman practice. The American naval vessels *Hornet, John Adams,* and *Alligator* also took turns in discouraging American merchant ships and skippers from continuing such trade.

With piracy and the slave trade finally under control around 1830, the United States Navy found time for exploration. In 1819 the American frigate *Congress* had achieved a great step forward by voyaging to the East Indies,

and ten years later the sloop *Vincennes* crossed the Pacific and then returned home by way of the Indian and Atlantic Oceans to become the first American man-of-war to span the Pacific and to circle the globe. Part of the purpose in such voyages was to impress foreign nations with American naval strength, and thus thwart raids on American merchant shipping. In 1835, the United States Navy established a regular East India Squadron to protect American interest in the farthest waters of the Pacific. Five years after its founding, the Squadron was placed under the command of Commodore Lawrence Kearny.

In October, 1842, Kearny made an important contribution to American expansion when he landed in China, with the U.S.S. *Constellation* and the U.S.S. *Boston,* to help reopen international trade. Then, four years later, Commodore James Biddle, who was acting as American Commissioner to China, attempted to carry the expansion a step further by extending friendly relationships to Japan. In July, 1846, he sailed to Yedo (now Tokyo) Bay, Japan, to negotiate a trade treaty with the Japanese. But the project was a failure. The Japanese were not ready for negotiations. And even as Biddle was sailing into Japan, America was experiencing serious difficulties with a much closer nation: Mexico.

The United States Navy's part in the Mexican War was completely one-sided, for Mexico had no official navy.

In the Mexican War, the Navy landed and operated six heavy guns at Veracruz (above) to aid the Army's bombardment of the city.

Navy sidewheelers steam up the Panuco River, capturing small Mexican gunboats and mopping up guerrilla bands in the jungles.

However, the war was important to naval history because of the development of landing and siege operations, which the Navy was to find of vital importance in later conflicts. The most outstanding of these was the siege of Veracruz, Mexico, a battle that lasted from March 9 to March 29, 1847. It had been decided that the only way to overcome Mexico quickly was to launch a combined Navy-Army as-

sault at the port of Veracruz, in the Gulf of Mexico. The Navy had to transport and land some 12,000 troops under General Winfield Scott, then cover the landings with gun support.

On March 9, the fighting troops were landing in a period of only five hours. The naval ships kept up a constant fire on the city's fortifications, not only to open up breaches in the walls, but to prevent the Mexicans from taking any effective action against the American troops. Even though the Mexicans had no ships at Veracruz, Navy units were often under heavy fire. On March 22 and March 23, Commander Josiah Tattnall led a small flotilla up under the guns of Castle San Juan de Ulloa, to pound the fort into submission. With the *Spitfire* and six other steamers he approached within 800 yards of the shore, where he remained for a half hour, firing continuously, while the enemy returned the fire heatedly, but with poor aim. This was the last major naval engagement in the Mexican War, though it was not until February, 1848, that the peace treaty was signed.

Emerging from the Mexican War was one naval figure who was to stand out in the era of American expansion: Matthew Calbraith Perry, younger brother of the famed hero of Lake Erie. Shortly after the Mexican conflict, American leaders began eyeing trade in the Far East again, and it was suggested that the Navy continue its diplomatic missions. Japan was considered the key to the situation, but the outlook was discouraging. It was well known that Japan had remained aloof, an isolated country since the early seventeenth century.

Finally, against this impregnable opponent, the United States dispatched Commodore Perry, with a special squadron. Perry was perhaps the only man in the entire country suitable for the assignment. Known as "the cast-iron commodore" and "Old Matt," he had a combination of astute imagination, high regard for tradition, and careful attention to detail.

"We will demand as a *right*, not solicit as a favor, those acts of courtesy due from one civilized nation to another," said Perry.

Some of the government officials in Washington were dubious. President Fillmore had prepared a special letter to the Emperor of Japan. Perry would carry this in an elaborate, hand-carved box of fragrant rosewood. And he requested that the letter and other official documents be inscribed on the finest vellum, embellished with government seals and ribbons. In the box were delicate gifts for the Emperor.

During the course of his two years of reading up on Japan, the Commodore was busy hand-picking the officers and men he wanted to accompany him. All of the ones who would come into close contact with the Japanese would be tall, formal in manner, and

distinctive in appearance.

Perry arrived at Yedo Bay on July 8, 1853, aboard his flagship, the side-wheeler *Susquehanna*. With her was another big, impressive side-wheeler, the *Mississippi* and two trim sloops, the *Plymouth* and *Saratoga*. The ships steamed slowly up the Bay and anchored off Uraga. Suddenly the warships were surrounded by a throng of small picket vessels, and a warning was issued to the Americans to leave at once. Perry ignored the warning. A Japanese officer now came alongside in a small boat and demanded to see the commanding officer.

"The Lord of the Forbidden Interior," he was politely told, "could not possibly demean his rank by appearing on deck to carry on a discussion."

This was the answer Perry had ordered and the crew was astonished to see that the Japanese took no affront.

Tattnall's flotilla—the Spitfire, Vixen, Bonita, Reefer, Petrel, Falcon, *and* Tampico—*bombard Castle San Juan de Ulloa at Veracruz.*

Instead, he seemed duly impressed. "We have the vice-governor of Uraga aboard," said the Japanese officer, "he is of very high rank."

"Why did you not bring the governor?" he was asked by the petty officer who was carrying on the liaison.

"He is forbidden to be on ships," came the answer. And would the Lord of the Forbidden Interior designate an officer whose rank was appropriate to conversing with a vice-governor?

Here is where the long months of selection and training were to prove themselves. Perry now sent, not a captain or commander, but a junior lieutenant. The lieutenant after a ceremonious greeting, announced that the expedition was a most honored one, for it bore a message from the President of the United States to the Emperor himself. Could the vice-governor see this message? *No one* was permitted to see it but the Emperor or one of his princes. However, if the governor himself would appear, he would be shown a *copy* of the letter.

A day later, after the vice-governor had retired to shore for a conference, the governor sailed out on an elaborately decorated barge. Now Perry, who had remained completely out of sight at all times, sent Captain Buchanan of his flagship to carry on the ceremonious negotiations at this level. The governor was impressed when he saw the rosewood box. Yet he hesitated. He was not certain that he would best be serving his Emperor by permitting foreigners to land to meet with members of the royal household.

"That would indeed be too bad," he was told, "for the Lord of the Forbidden Interior is committed to delivering the message, or dying in the attempt."

The governor carefully eyed the

tremendous guns of the ships, which had been purposely readied and exposed. Then, displaying no sign of emotion, he politely requested time to consult with the proper authorities, and returned to shore.

It was not until July 14 that Perry permitted himself to be seen. The Japanese had set up a fine pavilion on the shore, to which would come the Prince of Idzu, the properly ranked representative of the Emperor. The ships had all moved in closer to shore, where the Japanese could easily see that this mission of peace was well supported by the necessary engines of war. One hundred marines in well-starched dress uniforms had gone ashore and were lined up in procession with a company of seamen and two Navy bands.

At the proper moment, Perry appeared on the spotless deck of the *Susquehanna* in full dress, and was helped into his official barge to the sound of a thirteen-gun salute which echoed across the bay. Then, preceded by fifteen boats, each mounting a gun, the barge preceded at a dignified pace to the shore. The extent to which Perry had prepared and supervised each de-

The Japanese painting (above) shows two of Commodore Perry's four vessels anchored in Tokyo Bay in 1853. The steam frigate (right) is probably his flagship, the Susquehanna. *At the bottom of the opposite page, at extreme left, Perry goes ashore in Japan, followed by his negro standard-bearer. The second picture shows an American officer drilling a detachment of smartly-dressed Marines. In February, 1854, when Perry returned to arrange a trade treaty with Japan, some of his negro sailors (below, left) put on a minstrel show for Japanese officials on Perry's ship. The ten-year-old American invention, the telegraph, fascinated the Japanese, one of whom sketched one of the two instruments (right) which Perry presented to treaty officials.*

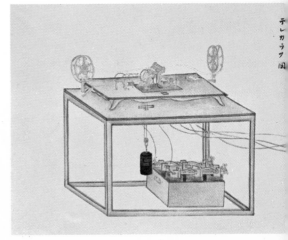

The wood-block print of a Japanese map at right pictures Commodore Matthew Calbraith Perry's fleet anchored in Yedo (now called Tokyo) Bay, Japan, on July 8, 1853. In the panel at left, the large ship at bottom is the American paddlewheel steamer Mississippi. *The procession of sailors (at top) marching briskly along behind a Navy band, with American flags flying, suggests that Perry's men seemed foreign indeed to the Japanese artist.*

This daguerreotype of Perry was made in 1848.

Perry as drawn by a Japanese artist in 1853.

tail was now seen at its best. As he stepped ashore, he was flanked by two superb looking negro seamen, the tallest, most impressive men he could find in the Navy. And in front of them marched two young midshipmen, bearing the rosewood box. To the Japanese, this pomp and pageantry signified that America was a nation worthy to carry on trade with Japan.

This meeting of Prince Idzu and the Commodore was not, however, the end of the negotiations. Perry was well aware that he could by no means ex-

pect an official answer to the request in the letter that trade be opened within a few days, or even weeks. "I shall return for an answer within six months," stated Perry solemnly.

In the United States, some newspapers severely criticized the Commodore, and suggested that the government attend to serious matters and discourage this type of "humbug." In February, 1854, the American Squadron returned. Further ceremonies took place. There were exchanges of gifts: for the Americans, silks and carvings and other Oriental handicrafts; for the Japanese, firearms, tools, clocks, and the most unusual item of all—a miniature railway with an engine which had a speed of twenty miles per hour.

Then the results of all this "humbug" were made clear. The Japanese, impressed with Perry's stratagem, and fully aware now of American naval strength, announced that they would sign the trade treaty. And thus it was that an inspired officer won the most important peacetime battle of the nineteenth century for the U.S. Navy.

Southerners on the rooftops at Charleston, South Carolina, watch as Confederate shore batteries bombard Fort Sumter, on the island (at center) in the middle of the harbor.

Heroes of
the Blue and Gray

"Fort Sumter has been shelled!"

Thus, on a mild spring day, April 12, 1861, was shattered the long era of peace which, since the War of 1812, had been disturbed only by minor conflicts far from American shores. And with the shelling of the Federal fort at Sumter by Confederates began one of the bitterest struggles in all history: the American Civil War. Many people do not think of the Civil War as a conflict in which the United States Navy played much of a part. Yet the outcome depended to a great extent on the successes and failures of the Federal Navy and the Confederate ships and guns that opposed it.

Gideon Welles, the Secretary of the Navy under Lincoln, clearly had an enormous job on his hands. Of the total of ninety ships in the United States Navy, only forty-two were ready for use when war broke out.

Most of the early battles were those of Union vessels against batteries stationed by the Confederates in strategic points along rivers and channels. At the end of May, 1861, the first action of any significance took place when Commander James Ward led a small flotilla of light river boats against a Confederate gun emplacement on the Potomac near Aquia Creek, Virginia. The Union boats accomplished little, since it was impossible to elevate the guns enough to knock out emplacements higher up on the hills.

Of considerably more importance was the Battle of Port Royal, South Carolina, in which a fleet of fourteen Union vessels under Flag Officer Samuel F. DuPont entered the sound between Fort Beauregard to the north and Fort Walker to the south. Ranging back and forth, the ships pounded the shore batteries into submission. It was a great loss for the South. Not only did the Federal ships have excellent Port Royal Harbor as a supply station, but their success proved that the finest forts ashore were vulnerable to the guns of the U.S. Navy.

This was a great period of trial and error for both sides. On February 6, 1862, Lt. Seth Phelps set out with three gunboats, the *Conestoga*, *Tyler*, and *Lexington*, to proceed up the Tennessee River to disrupt Confederate operations. During the next four days, Phelps went as far as Florence, Alabama, forced the enemy to burn six transport steamers loaded with supplies, captured two other steamers before they could be scuttled, and

"Cayuga."

brought back the hull of the half-finished gunboat *Eastport*.

All of these exploits were to prove invaluable experience in preparing for an important naval campaign in the spring of 1862. Among the officers of the U.S. Navy, Flag Officer David Glasgow Farragut was making a name for himself. It was decided that he would make a try at capturing the vital city of New Orleans from the Southerners, and in mid-April he assembled his fleet: one screw frigate, four screw sloops, a paddle-wheeler, twelve gunboats, and twenty schooners. First he had to navigate through the Head of the Passes (just at the spot in the Delta where the Mississippi splits into four channels and flows into the Gulf of Mexico). Then, a few miles upriver, he would encounter a log barrier stretched across the river, Fort Jackson on the left bank and Fort St. Philip

on the right. The former was a relatively modern fortification built by army engineers, and the latter an old Spanish fort, both reinforced by the South with extra guns. Beyond that there would be waiting units of the Confederate fleet.

On April 16, the fleet had advanced to a position three miles below the forts, and Farragut ordered his advance units to commence pounding the bulwarks. For five days the Union ships kept up a steady fire, to no avail. Then, on the night of April 20, Farragut dispatched his fleet captain, Henry H. Bell, upriver to destroy the chain-and-log barrier, and the small raiding expedition managed to make enough of a gap for ships to go through in a single file.

Just after midnight on April 24, the fleet was ready to make the dangerous dash past the forts. Each ship's crew

David G. Farragut

David D. Porter

The ship at center is Commodore Theodorus Bailey's Cayuga, anchored near the levee at New Orleans on April 29, 1862, the day the city was surrendered.

had spent the preceding days in packing logs, sand bags, mattresses, and anything else they could lay hands on around boilers and other vital areas where a hit could disable their ships. With this makeshift armor, the fleet proceeded, now arranged in three divisions: 1) Commodore Bailey, with two warships and six gunboats; 2) Farragut in his flagship *Hartford,* with the *Brooklyn* and *Richmond;* and 3) Bell with one warship and five gunboats. The remainder of the ships—the sloop *Portsmouth,* and twenty mortar boats under Commander David D. Porter—were to remain below the barrier to lend support later on. At 2:00 A.M., the fleet got underway.

Captain Bailey's leading vessel, the fast gunboat *Cayuga,* reached the barrier at about 3:40 A.M. and bore the initial brunt of the fire from the forts. In the half hour it took her to get out of the firing range of the forts, she received more than forty hits. Then she plunged into the midst of the Confederate defensive fleet with guns blasting madly. The two warships *Pensacola* and *Mississippi* came next, where they were immediately attacked by the Confederate ironclad *Manassas.* Soon the flagship *Hartford* was in the thick of the battle, too.

During the battle, the Union ships received repeated hits, yet all managed to get through except three of the gunboats, and the *Portsmouth* and Porter's mortar boats, which were supposed to remain downstream in position. Now, safely upriver and out of range of the forts, Farragut's remaining ships peppered the inferior Confederate defense fleet, knocking out a dozen vessels, including the plucky *Manassas.* The Confederate ironclad had continued fighting to the end. The next day, Farragut

Farragut's fleet runs the gantlet between Forts Jackson (left foreground) and St. Philip (

reat Union victory occurred below New Orleans on the Mississippi River, on April 24, 1862.

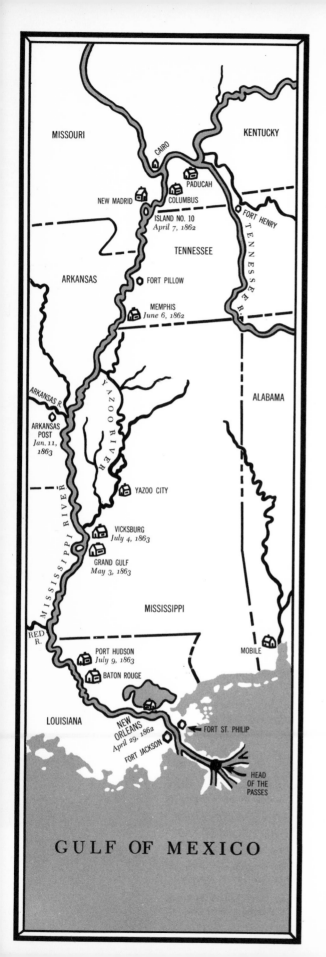

MISSOURI

KENTUCKY

CAIRO

PADUCAH

NEW MADRID

COLUMBUS

ISLAND NO. 10
April 7, 1862

FORT HENRY

TENNESSEE

ARKANSAS

FORT PILLOW

MEMPHIS
June 6, 1862

TENNESSEE R.

ARKANSAS R.

YAZOO RIVER

ALABAMA

ARKANSAS
POST
*Jan. 11,
1863*

YAZOO CITY

MISSISSIPPI RIVER

VICKSBURG
July 4, 1863

GRAND GULF
May 3, 1863

MISSISSIPPI

RED
R.

PORT HUDSON
July 9, 1863

MOBILE

BATON ROUGE

LOUISIANA

NEW
ORLEANS
April 29, 1862

FORT ST. PHILIP

FORT JACKSON

HEAD
OF THE
PASSES

GULF OF MEXICO

anchored off New Orleans. By April 29, the Union flag was flying over the city and the two river forts had capitulated.

This fine tribute to Farragut's skill was to be followed by one of the most ridiculously expensive campaigns—in men and in supplies—in naval history. The Navy Department now gave him orders to attempt a campaign about which he had grave doubts: to cruise up the Mississippi still farther and attack such Confederate strongholds as Vicksburg, Mississippi. Farragut already knew what the problems would be. The river was treacherous for sea-going vessels. At every bend in the river, the South would have strong artillery units to rake the river with shot. Besides, explained Farragut, thousands of Union troops would be needed to hold whatever positions he could knock out with his naval guns.

But Washington persisted, and the end of May found Farragut bearing slowly northward on Vicksburg, with two-thirds of his ships already damaged, either by the enemy or by natural obstructions. Even so, towards the end of June, Farragut had managed the "impossible" — taking the *Hartford* and seven other ships right past the batteries at Vicksburg—but Vicksburg could not be taken.

If Farragut had been dauntless in his efforts, the South was to be just as

This map shows the major Confederate strongholds on the Mississippi River, and gives the dates on which they fell to the Union.

much so. On July 15, Union officers and men were surprised to witness a gray shape charging downriver into their midst and right past their ships. It was the Confederate ironclad *Arkansas,* which had risked a dash from a hide-out to the north, up the Yazoo River, to put in at Vicksburg, where she would not only be under the defense of shore guns, but could harass the Northern warships.

By late 1862, General Grant had arrived on the scene, in answer to Farragut's demands for army support on land, and was attacking the Vicksburg area. But the winter of 1862-63 saw one Union failure after another. It was almost impossible to ferry troops back and forth by ship because the riverbanks lay under range of Confederate guns. It was equally impossible for the men to march to strategic points along the river because the Mississippi was bordered by so many treacherous swamps. Grant himself conceived of what sounded like a logical idea to help the situation, as far as the Navy was concerned. The Mississippi at Vicksburg was shaped like a gigantic "U," with the city and its heaviest batteries at the curve. Why not cut a canal across the top part of this "U" and bypass the city entirely? After much time and labor were expended, it was found that the tough clay soil was impossible to dig with equipment at hand, and the project was abandoned.

It was not until July 4, 1863, that Vicksburg finally fell to the North after a six-week siege in which the city was bombarded unmercifully. But Grant had to maneuver some 30,000 troops to accomplish the victory, with Admirals Farragut and Porter ranging up and down the river bombarding shore emplacements at great cost to their own men and ships. The battle was over, but not the memory of the incredible effort that had gone into it.

The tragedy of the Confederate Navy was not that it lacked experienced officers and brave seamen, but that it had to rely on a pitifully small number of true war vessels, and a large number of makeshift ones. The struggle might have been even more lopsided had the South not had the services of dedicated men like Stephen R. Mallory, the Confederate Secretary of the Navy. As early as the spring of 1861, for example, when the Union blockade began, Mallory had suggested armored vessels, to make up in invulnerability what the South lacked in numbers. On May 10 of that year he recommended to the Naval Committee: "I regard the possession of an iron-armored ship as a matter of the first necessity." As a start, he had the hull of the half-burned Union vessel *Merrimac* at the Norfolk Navy Yard hauled into drydock, where an iron superstructure was built on top of her. Renamed the *Virginia,* she was expected to be able to run the blockade without being sunk.

When word reached the North that this odd craft was being built, the Union Navy promptly sent a representative to marine engineer John Ericsson,

Island No. 10, a Confederate fort on the Kentucky-Tennessee border (see map below) on the Mississippi, finally surrendered to the Navy on April 7, 1862, after a month-long campaign. The picture (above) shows its bombardment by Union ironclads (left) and mortar boats (right).

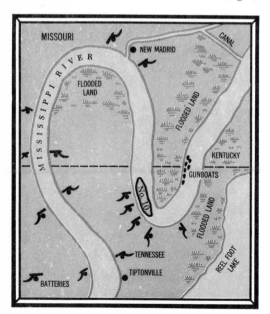

who had invented the screw propeller. Could he design an ironclad for the North? He not only could, but he had an old design already in his files—for the strange "cheesebox on a raft" that was to become the U.S.S. *Monitor*.

The *Virginia* and the *Monitor* were thus completed at about the same time, in February, 1862. But the *Virginia* was the first to see action. On March 8, she steamed from the Norfolk Navy Yard at 11:00 A.M., and headed down the Elizabeth River towards the anchorage at Hampton Roads, where two blockaders had long been stationed, the U.S.S. *Cumberland* and the U.S.S. *Congress*. Outside the bar of the bay lay three other Union vessels: *Minnesota*, *Roanoke*, and *St. Lawrence*.

The *Virginia* plodded onward as the

Cumberland readied her guns. Time after time the Union vessel's guns blasted away, but the shot merely bounced off the sloping iron sides. The *Virginia* fired a few rounds with her bow pivot gun, but her real intent was to pierce the enemy with her cast-iron ram at the bow.

"Prepare to ram!" barked the captain, Flag Officer Franklin Buchanan.

The *Virginia* plowed into the side of the sloop, and within minutes the *Cumberland* was on her way to the bottom. The *Virginia* now headed for the *Congress,* which she began to pepper with cannon fire, as the helpless Union vessel—though possessing fifty guns—was unable to inflict any damage at all on her opponent. With the captain, Lt. Joseph Smith, killed, and most

At Vicksburg, Mississippi (above) Admiral Porter's fleet ran past the city's guns on the night of April 16, 1863, after work on the bypass canal (below) had to be abandoned. This move allowed Grant to attack the city from the south, and to capture it on July 4, 1863.

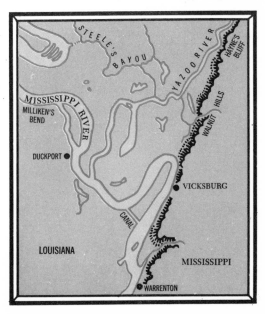

of the crew slaughtered, the *Congress* raised a white flag of surrender.

History was steaming south that day and the following night in the form of another ironclad, the *Monitor*, from the North. And it was well she was on her way, for the easy victories of the *Virginia* (still referred to in the North by her old name *Merrimac*) had literally struck panic into the Union fleet. All night long tugboats pulled frantically at the *Minnesota* (which had run aground while trying to help the *Cumberland* and the *Congress*), trying to free her before the monster could return and blast her to eternity.

The *Monitor* almost failed to get to Hampton Roads at all. Caught in a gale en route from New York, she leaked so badly that "the water came down the turret like a waterfall." The fires almost went out in the engine room, and asphyxiated crewmen had to be taken topside to be revived time after time during the ordeal. The *Monitor* reached Chesapeake Bay, off Hampton Roads, in the late afternoon of March 8, in time to hear the distant sound of cannon, but not in time to participate in the battle. By midnight, her skipper, Lt. John L. Worden, had brought her alongside the grounded *Minnesota*.

In the early dawn of March 9, the *Virginia* approached from Sewell's Point, commanded now by Lt. Catesby Jones, whose intended victim was the *Minnesota*. When about two miles

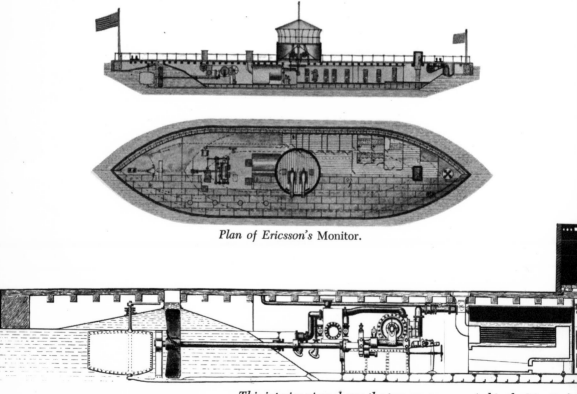

Plan of Ericsson's Monitor.

This interior view shows the two cannons carried in the Monitor's t away, his lookout noticed something strange.

Jones peered through the glasses. "Looks like an immense shingle," he muttered, "with a cheesebox on top."

At a distance of one mile, Jones opened fire on the motionless *Minnesota*. At that moment, Lt. Worden, inside the *Monitor*, gave his orders.

"Half speed ahead," he said.

The little *Monitor* moved out into the bay, her tired crew now excited into action, despite the fact that no one

John Ericsson

Stephen R. Mallory

Gideon Welles

When United States Secretary of the Navy Gideon Welles learned that Confederate Secretary Mallory was building ironclads, he persuaded Ericsson to design the Monitor *for the Union. Her swivel turret wore 8-inch armor.*

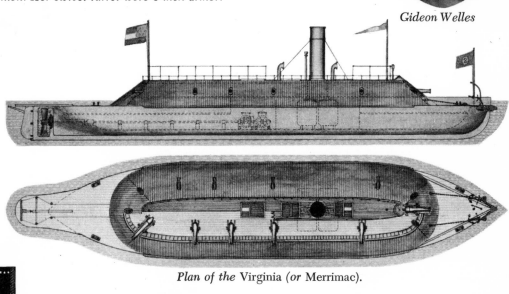

Plan of the Virginia (*or* Merrimac).

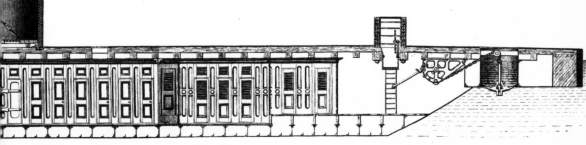

s 172 feet long, weighed 776 tons, and ran at a speed of 7 knots.

On March 8, 1862, Confederate Flag Officer Buchanan's ironclad Virginia (Merrimac) rammed the U.S.S. Cumberland (above). Lieutenant G.U. Morris of the Cumberland refused to surrender and his ship went down with colors flying. Next day, off Norfolk, Virginia, the Union ship Monitor (below) fought her famous battle with the Virginia.

had slept in more than two days. Her two guns, new 11-inch Dahlgrens, were stripped for action.

The *Virginia* now concentrated her fire on this new menace, but Lt. Catesby Jones was dismayed to find that his gunners could scarcely make a hit, and when they did, the shot bounced off with no damage to the "cheesebox." So he next resorted to the tactics that had been so successful the day before: ramming. In the first attempt, the *Virginia's* bow passed right over the *Monitor's* deck, the sharp edges of which bit into the Confederate vessel's hull and caused a slight leak. Jones abandoned this method and soon began firing again.

The battle lasted four hours. The *Monitor* was struck twenty-two times, but with no damage. In return she fired almost fifty rounds at the *Virginia*, and succeeded in cracking the outer layer of iron in several places, and toppling the *Virginia's* smokestack.

Finally, the *Virginia* retired from battle. The contest was a draw, and the *Virginia* was never to see battle again. In a short time, the Confederates were forced to abandon Norfolk and the valiant *Virginia* was destroyed to prevent capture.

But the South was far from through on the seas. The ingenuity of the South's naval engineers, intensified by the urgency of her cause, might still have worked victory out of sure defeat had certain developments been properly backed and pushed to completion earlier in the war.

There is, for example, the remarkable story of the *Hunley*.

In the Confederate stronghold of Charleston, South Carolina, closely blockaded by the naval units of Union Admirals DuPont and Dahlgren in the middle of 1863, plans were evolved for a new type of vessel. This class was to be made up of old gunboats, called "Davids," cut close to the waterline, covered with iron plating, and armed with a 100-pound charge of gunpowder affixed at the end of a long spar at the bow. The plan was to ram a Union vessel hard enough so that the spar would stick, like a spear, then back off 100 feet and set off the explosive by yanking a long cord attached to the detonator.

After a few disastrous failures, it was proved that the plan *would* work when a "David" was sent against the Union ship *New Ironsides* during the night of October 5. The explosive was driven into the enemy and set off, severely damaging the hull. In the confusion, the "David" escaped. And, even as she was being readied for further forays, another more sinister vessel lay waiting along the Charleston docks. This was the *Hunley*, a vessel inspired by the "Davids," but built to *submerge* as a submarine. She was constructed from a 25-foot section of iron boiler, four feet wide and about six feet deep. The bow and stern were pointed, and each contained a ballast tank which could be filled to make the vessel submerge, and pumped out to make her rise. On the top was a small conning tower

This map (which places North at bottom) locates Hampton Roads. Where the James enters Chesapeake Bay, the ironclads battled. The Cumberland sank off Newport News.

Captain of the Virginia, Franklin Buchanan.

which was only about fifteen inches high. Through four tiny glass observation ports, the captain could see where he was going. Power was supplied by eight men who sat inside the craft and turned a crankshaft with their arms. This was attached to a propeller at the stern. The tactics were to be the same as in the "David's" attack: approach the enemy at night; plunge a spar into the hull; back off and discharge an explosive. There was one important difference however. When several hundred feet from the enemy, the Hunley would submerge, thus avoiding detection.

The night of February 17, 1864, was clear and cloudless as the Hunley moved out of Breach Inlet, near Charleston Harbor, and headed seaward. Her target was the Union blockader Housatonic. The time was 8:00 P.M. When the Hunley had moved close enough to the Housatonic so there was danger of being spotted, her commander, Lt. George E. Dixon, gave his men a rest and commenced the tricky maneuver of flooding the bow and stern tanks. Within a few minutes the Hunley had submerged so that nothing at all remained above the surface except about ten inches of the tiny conning tower.

A little before 9:00 P.M., officers on the deck of the Housatonic felt a strange thud against the hull. An alarm was sounded and within seconds, the decks resounded with the drumbeat of many feet as other officers and seamen raced to their posts. But it was

Lieutenant John L. Worden (center, wearing eyeglasses) photographed with his crew on the deck of the Monitor. Worden's eyes were injured following a direct hit on the pilot house.

too late. When the *Hunley* had almost reached the *Housatonic,* she had gone just under water, then lunged forward as fast as the men could crank her, to plunge the spar firmly into the enemy's hull. Lt. Dixon had reached his target. But as the men reversed the crank and moved furiously to reverse the *Hunley,* something went wrong. The gunpowder charge exploded prematurely with a tremendous blast.

It took only four minutes for the *Housatonic* to go down. Lt. George Dixon and his brave crew had completed an historical achievement. But he was never to realize it. For even as the blockader went down, she carried the little *Hunley* and her entire crew with her to her grave—the first undersea boat to sink an enemy in battle.

Strange though some of the battles of the Civil War were—often fought between bizarre vessels of types never seen before, or between a mixture of land and sea forces—there were from time to time important naval battles in which one authentic ship of war attacked another. Such was the famous engagement between the U.S.S. *Kearsarge* and the C.S.S. *Alabama.* The only strange aspect of this battle was

OVERLEAF: *This dramatic picture incorrectly shows the* Cumberland *sinking on the same day as the battle of the* Monitor *and* Virginia.

85

Rear Admiral John A. B. Dahlgren (left) built the Navy's first ordnance laboratory at the Washington Navy Yard, and invented 9- and 11-inch cannon, called "Dahlgrens," before the start of the Civil War. Dahlgren replaced Admiral Du Pont as commander of the squadron blockading Charleston in 1863, and was present when a "David" damaged the Union ship New Ironsides. He quickly saw the menace of the "Davids" (forerunners of submarines) although many officers ridiculed them. The two types of Civil War cannon shown here include the Parrott gun (above) used by North and South alike on ships and harbor fortifications. It was one of the first to throw an explosive shell; but it might also burst, as this one did, aboard the U.S.S. Susquehanna, in 1865. The Dahlgren gun (below) was less likely to explode as its walls were "pressure curved" or thickened to resist internal stresses. Dahlgrens were nicknamed "Soda bottles."

that it was fought thousands of miles away from Civil War battlefields, off the northern coast of France.

The *Alabama* was a fine, fast Confederate raider which had effectively attacked Federal shipping for almost two years when she finally met the *Kearsarge* in June, 1864. She was 220 feet long, with a 32-foot beam, barkentine-rigged, with extra-tall masts, and with an engine that could drive her almost 15 knots through the water whenever she chose to use both sail and steam during a chase. Under Captain Raphael Semmes, she started her career harassing Union whaling vessels near the Azores, making a total of nine captures in this sector alone. Semmes then sailed to Labrador, burning a large grain ship, the *Brilliant*, after which he moved into the Caribbean where Union warships were warned to be on the lookout for him.

In January, 1863, the *Alabama* was boldly slipping in toward the blockaded port of Galveston when she was sighted by the U.S.S. *Hatteras*. As dusk was falling, the *Hatteras* steamed away from the other blockaders to check the identity of the stranger. But, before she knew it, the *Alabama* had attacked the smaller vessel, which was an old side-wheeler. Shots ripped apart the awkward "walking beams" which moved the paddle wheels, and the captain had to surrender. The dashing Captain Semmes transported his newly taken prisoners to Jamaica, then headed for other waters before the Union blockaders could take after him.

For seventeen months more the *Alabama* ranged the far waters all the way from the African coast to the Far East and back to Europe. On June 11, 1864, the trim Confederate entered the harbor at Cherbourg, France, badly in need of repairs, refueling, and an overhaul of her barnacle-encrusted bottom. She had already run up a remarkable record against the North: one warship sunk and more than sixty merchant vessels captured, most of which were stripped and burned.

But time was running out. No sooner was the *Alabama* reported at the French port than word was sent to Captain John A. Winslow, skipper of the U.S.S. *Kearsarge*, farther up the coast, off the Netherlands. The *Kearsarge*, a vessel much like the *Alabama* in size and speed, steamed immediately to Cherbourg, where she anchored off the harbor mouth, leaving no doubt about her intention to intercept the enemy. The dauntless Captain Raphael Semmes was equal to the occasion.

"I will be out to fight within two days," he announced, as soon as he could effect some makeshift repairs.

At 10:15 A.M. on Sunday, June 19, the *Alabama* sailed proudly out of the port. By this time, the word had spread through the city that a battle was to take place, and a large part of the population lined the highest bluffs along the shore to watch.

The day was mild and sunny. As soon as the *Kearsarge* spotted her opponent she headed for the *Alabama*. The Confederate vessel opened fire

The Confederacy's most powerful ram, the ironclad Tennessee (above) surrendered to Farragut after fighting fiercely in the Battle of Mobile Bay.

Off Charleston in 1864, the South's tiny Hunley (right)—the first submarine ever to destroy an enemy ship—sank the Union steam sloop Housatonic.

This interior view of the Hunley was painted by an unknown Union soldier. Only eight men—not eleven as shown here—turned the ship's crankshaft.

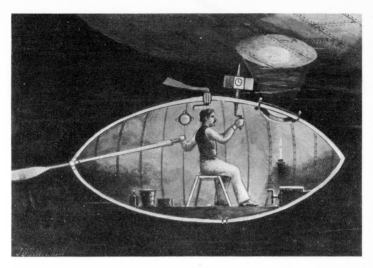

The first submarine used in combat was not the Civil War's Hunley, but the Turtle (above) designed by David Bushnell during the American Revolution. The one-man Turtle is shown here probably trying to blow up the British Eagle, off New York in 1776. The submarine had to retreat before she could attach a bomb to the Eagle's hull.

The illustration (below) shows a side view and a plan of the gun deck of the Union gunboat Benton. Admiral Porter commanded the Benton in his dash (see page 79) past the batteries at Vicksburg.

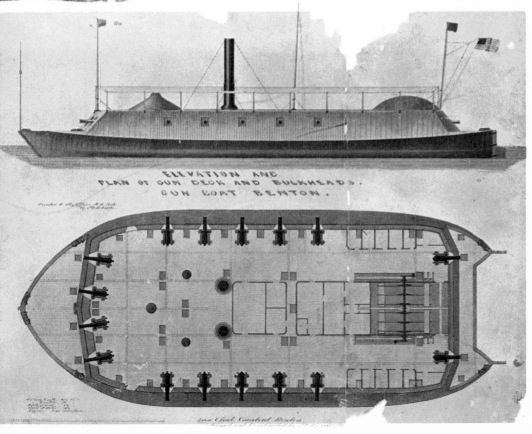

ELEVATION AND
PLAN OF GUN DECK AND BULKHEADS.
GUN BOAT BENTON.

*Raphael Semmes
of the* Alabama

*John A. Winslow
of the* Kearsarge

first with a full broadside from her starboard guns. A few shots rattled through the rigging. Captain Winslow held his fire and moved in closer. The *Alabama* fired a second broadside, this one with more effect, but doing no major damage.

"Hold your fire," Winslow ordered.

The *Kearsarge* steamed closer. It was evident that the *Alabama* was clearing her guns for a third round. Then, at about 900 yards, Winslow gave the order to fire.

For an hour the two vessels ranged in a series of circles about each other. Right from the start, it was evident that the *Kearsarge* held one vital advantage: the North's ammunition was far superior to that of the South. The South could not manufacture a sufficient amount of ammunition for her own needs and had to rely on blockade runners to bring in supplies from Europe and Latin America. Time after time, Semmes' gunners made vital hits, only to have the shells fail to explode,

leaving the *Kearsarge* undamaged.

The Union vessel had still another advantage: two 11-inch Dahlgren guns, which lobbed shells into the *Alabama* with deadly accuracy. Captain Semmes bravely continued the fight for more than an hour, by which time many of his crew were casualties, the hull was riddled, and most of the *Alabama's* guns had been silenced.

"We will try to make shore before we sink," said Semmes dejectedly to his remaining officers, "we can no longer fight back."

But it was too late. Much of the rigging had been shot away; the ship no longer responded to her wheel; and an 11-inch Dahlgren shell had pierced the engine room to blast apart her engines and boilers. As the *Alabama* started to sink, Winslow thoughtfully sent one of his two lifeboats to pick up survivors. However, the North was to be beaten out of absolute victory, for Captain Semmes boldly hailed a nearby English yacht, the *Deerhound*, which had come out to watch the contest. Aboard this, he and forty-one men escaped to England, thus avoiding capture by going to neutral territory. The *Alabama* had finally lost a battle; but in return she had wiped out $6,547,000 worth of Union shipping and supplies in her twenty-two-month career.

Captain Winslow returned home a hero, and the *Kearsarge* was commended for having finally struck a damaging blow against the South. Strangely enough, even at this late date in the war, there had been a great deal of bitterness in the North because the Confederacy had inflicted some notable losses on the Union in the spring of 1864, and particularly during April and May. A strange Southern vessel named the *Albemarle,* a small ironclad with only two guns and a ram at her bow, had played havoc with a Union force, sinking the converted ferryboat *Southfield,* severely damaging the gunboat *Miami,* and putting two others to flight in a single engagement. In a later battle, the little ironclad had been attacked by an entire flotilla; the repaired gunboat *Miami,* three "double-enders," and three armed steamers. She had not only managed to hold off all of these assailants, but had placed a shell squarely in the boiler room of one, the *Sassacus,* before retiring with one of her two guns knocked out.

The North had fared badly too in the Red River campaign, which had been so badly conceived and executed that ships were actually sent upriver to objectives which they could never reach because of the excessive draft required for their hulls. The only thing which saved the North at this discour-

aging point in naval affairs was that the South was feeling the great pinch of the blockade.

With this weird, confused, and highly diversified background of naval operations during the course of more than three bitter years, the Civil War moved into the summer of 1864. And naval history was about to take a giant step at a place called Mobile Bay.

The story begins somewhat earlier, in the summer of 1863. During the months from July on, units of the Northern fleet under Rear Admiral John A. Dahlgren had been regularly engaged in pounding the defenses of various forts in and around Charleston, South Carolina. Dahlgren, a naval engineer and inventor of the gun bearing his name, found victories hard to come by in the face of stubborn Confederate resistance. But the North was gaining valuable experience in the use of naval guns against land-based artillery, and some of this experience was put to good use when, in July, 1864, Admiral David Glasgow Farragut prepared to attack Mobile, Alabama.

Mobile was a strategic port for the South, so much so that both the city and the harbor were more heavily de-

The British blockade runner Thistle.

On Sunday morning, June 19, 1864, the Alabama *sailed out of the harbor at Cherbourg, France, into the English Channel, and began her battle with the U.S.S.* Kearsarge. *A gun crew on the* Kearsarge *is shown above. Below, the victorious* Kearsarge *(right) rescues the survivors of the sinking* Alabama.

fended, mile for mile, than any other position along the entire Confederate coast line. At the outer entrances to the bay, three strong forts were established: Fort Powell to the west, with six guns; Fort Gaines in the center, on Dauphin Island, with twenty-six guns; and the largest, Fort Morgan, with twenty-three heavy and forty-six light guns, at Mobile Point. Mobile Point was the thin arm that protected the main harbor, and most vessels had to pass through the channel directly under the guns of Fort Morgan to enter Mobile Bay.

In addition to the lines of earthworks and batteries along the bay, the harbor entrance had been all but closed by rows of heavy pilings stretching from Dauphin Island two-thirds of the way across. Where these ended, the Confederate Navy had laid a heavy mine field, containing almost 200 "torpedoes" (as mines were called at the time). This left but one safe passageway for ships.

Admiral Farragut's plan was a daring one. He would lead his fleet right through this narrow entrance, at full speed and while the tide was flooding the bay. For an attacking force he would take four heavy sloops and three light ones, each one with a gunboat lashed to the port side, to serve as shields against the fort's guns and to be used in battle once inside the bay. These fourteen vessels were all of wood. However, Farragut did have four ironclads, which would run in close to the fort, to draw fire away from the more vulnerable wooden ships, and to knock out as many of the shore guns as possible. Two of these, the *Tecumseh* and the *Manhattan*, were 190 feet long, with a single turret that mounted two 15-inch guns. The other two, *Winnebago* and *Chickasaw*, were about 65 feet longer, and each had two turrets and a total of four 11-inch guns.

In mid-July, as preparations were under way, Farragut ordered his wooden vessels to take the following steps as protection: strip all unnecessary spars, rigging, and deck equipment; put up splinter nets on the starboard side (the one that would be exposed to fire from the fort); lay sand bags around the decks to protect all vital machinery, the helm, and other critical points; and use sails, hammocks, and other material to protect the helmsman from flying splinters.

On the night of August 4, Farragut's fleet lay off Mobile Bay. There was no doubt that the Confederate defenders were ready and confident that the Union vessels would be destroyed as they steamed within range of Fort Morgan's 69 guns. Waiting, too, for any ship that did pass the suicidal run through the bottleneck was the Confederate *Tennessee*.

The *Tennessee*, which the South considered its "most powerful" ironclad, was a new and improved version of the famed *Virginia (Merrimac)*. Though she was some 50 feet shorter, she had heavier armor than any previous ironclad, had a strong, armored ram at the bow, and carried two seven-inch and four six-inch guns. In places, her armor was as much as six inches thick, considered impenetrable by the heaviest guns in Admiral Farragut's fleet. As an escort, the *Tennessee* had three wooden gunboats, the *Gaines*, *Morgan*, and *Selma*. Judging by the havoc the earlier ironclad, *Virginia* had wreaked on the *Cumberland* and *Congress* at Hampton Roads, it looked as though the *Tennessee* could destroy the Union fleet in short order.

By six o'clock the following morning, August 5, the fourteen wooden ships of the Union fleet were moving forward with the flood tide, two abreast, while the four heavy and awkward ironclads struggled to maintain the lead. Time after time, Farragut noticed with concern, the wooden ships threatened to overtake the ironclads, and Farragut had to halt the vessels in the rear. What he could not see was the mounting temperature inside the ironclads as the engines were pushed to the limit. The temperature in the engine rooms was over 125 degrees and the men had to be relieved constantly, or taken on deck to revive after they had passed out.

As Fort Morgan opened up on the invading armada, the ironclad *Tecumseh* moved into the lead, according to Farragut's plan, followed by her sister ironclads *Manhattan*, *Winnebago*, and *Chickasaw*. It was 7:00 A.M. and the battle was officially under way.

Admiral Farragut, on the bridge of his flagship *Hartford*, climbed into the rigging so he could better direct operations. Ahead, he saw the four ironclads approach the fort, where they received a deluge of fire at close range. Just ahead of the *Hartford* was the lead warship *Brooklyn*, lashed to the gunboat *Octorara*. Attached to his own vessel was the gunboat *Metacomet*. And astern in the procession came the *Richmond*, lashed to the *Port Royal*, the *Lackawanna* with the *Seminole*, the *Monongahela* with the *Kennebec*, the *Ossipee* with the *Itasca*, and the *Oneida* with the *Galena*.

Suddenly, as he watched, disaster struck hard and fast. At 7:20, as the *Tecumseh* approached the narrow channel, the enemy ironclad *Tennessee* appeared from behind Mobile Point to the east and steamed directly at the invader. Commander Tunis A. M. Craven of the Union ship saw the enemy coming and swerved slightly in order to prepare to meet the attack. In so doing he moved his vessel too far to the west—right into the edge of the mine field. There followed a tremendous explosion and within half a minute the *Tecumseh* had gone to the bottom.

In the tiny pilot house, Commander Craven knew that his ship was doomed the instant the explosion rocked the vessel from stem to stern. Yet he turned calmly to John Collins, the pilot, and motioned to the escape ladder.

"After you, pilot," he said, "I leave my ship last."

Collins scrambled free of the sinking ship and was later rescued. But Commander Craven was never seen again. With him went 93 of a crew of 114.

The sinking of the *Tecumseh,* however, was less serious than the further disaster which now suddenly threatened the Union ships. All at once the lead ship, *Brooklyn,* was seen to slow down, and from the churning water around her it was evident that she was going into reverse. Farragut stared for a few seconds in horrified disbelief. While in motion, at full speed and with the pull of the tide, the fleet had some chance of running through the guns of the fort. But to stop dead in the water, at close range, would be suicide.

"What is wrong?" he barked from his high perch in the *Hartford's* rigging.

"Torpedoes, sir," came the answer from the deck. The *Brooklyn* had sighted mines directly ahead, and was frantically signaling to turn back.

Now Farragut was faced with the most important decision of his career. To continue ahead seemed certain disaster. Yet to turn back would mean the end of the battle.

For an instant he hesitated. Then his voice rang out loudly and clearly above the noises of battle.

"Damn the torpedoes!"

Then he directed orders at Captains Jouett of the gunboat alongside and Drayton of the *Hartford:* "Four bells!

Captain Drayton, go ahead! Jouett, full speed!"

Farragut now had his ship swung, not to the east toward the open water of the channel, but slightly to the west —right over the mine field. His alarmed officers could see the ominous black shadows of the mines, right under the hull of the ship. And those closer to the waterline could actually hear the sound of the wooden hull striking the metal primers of the mines. But not a single explosion occurred. The *Hartford* steamed swiftly forward, to be followed by the *Brooklyn* and the others in the battle line.

Now the *Tennessee,* under the command of the South's senior naval officer, Admiral Franklin Buchanan, was in the center of battle, attempting— though futilely—to ram one of the attacking wooden ships. Buchanan was a scrappy fighter who cared little that the odds were heavily against him.

This map shows the forts and minefields at the entrance to Mobile Bay, and the course of invasion of Admiral David G. Farragut's vessels on the morning of August 5, 1864.

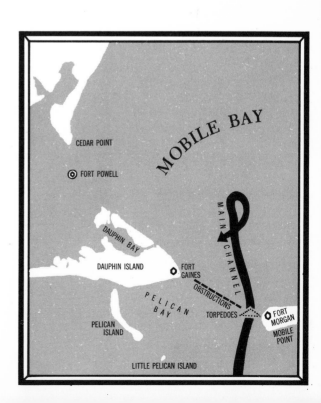

As Farragut's fleet runs past Fort Morgan on Mobile Bay, the Confederate ram Tennessee *(left foreground) steams forward to attack.*

His objective was to keep the Union ships stopped near the entrance, where the fort's guns could continue to pound them. But his vessel was far too slow. The *Monongahela* and *Lackawanna,* closest at the time to the Confederate ironclad, not only managed to escape being rammed, but in turn rammed the *Tennessee,* inflicting some damage to her hull. Next the *Hartford* managed to unleash a full broadside at the *Tennessee.* By this time, the battle had been carried by the tide, as well as the engines of the Union ships, some four miles past the entrance to Mobile Bay, and well out of range of the batteries at Fort Morgan.

In relatively open water, with no shore support, the *Tennessee* could not hope to win. Besides, one of her three supporting gunboats had been sunk, a second one captured, and the third all but forced out of action. But "Old Buck"—Admiral Buchanan—refused to surrender. The *Tennessee's* steering chains were shot away, so she could barely maneuver. Her smokestack had been toppled, so the interior of the ship was thick with fumes and smoke. And her gun shutters had been so jammed from the fire of Union ships that she was finally unable to fire her own guns in defense. Nevertheless, she continued in action, charging at full speed through the Northern fleet

in an attempt to ram her enemies.

Finally, at 10:00 A.M. that day, with the U.S.S. *Chickasaw* hanging onto the *Tennessee's* tail and pounding her mercilessly with her 11-inchers, Admiral Buchanan surrendered. He himself had been wounded, and half the crew killed or put out of action. And there was little left of what had a few hours earlier been the pride of the Confederate Navy.

It had been a costly battle for the North, "the most desperate battle I

ever fought" reported Farragut later, with some 315 casualties in the Union fleet. But the Battle of Mobile Bay, in effect, marked the end of the Confederate Navy. Within a few days, all of the forts had surrendered to the joint Army-Navy action of the North. From then on, the South was unable to put on any show of naval strength.

When the Civil War ended with Lee's surrender at Appomattox in April, 1865, the Union Navy had more than 600 ships, of which about 60 had some armor, including a number of well-armored monitors, and a considerable number of gunboats with some armor protection in vital places. In addition, there were 57,900 officers and men. This represented a tremendous growth when compared with the 90 vessels and 9,000 officers and men at the start of the war. This fact in itself remains as important evidence that the United States Navy played a vital part in winning the War between the States.

"Remember the MAINE!"

Cuba, Spain's most important remaining colony in the New World, had become increasingly dissatisfied with Spanish rule. Just before the turn of the century, there were a number of revolutionary uprisings in the colony. On January 25, 1898, the United States battleship *Maine* sailed into Havana harbor to protect American citizens living in Cuba if the dispute between Cuban revolutionaries and the Spanish rulers became serious. The United States had already given unofficial encouragement to the revolutionaries and had offered to mediate the dispute. On February 15, 1898, without warning, the *Maine,* still lying at anchor in Havana harbor, was blown up with a loss of two hundred and sixty men. No one has ever discovered who blew up the ship. But the United States assumed that Spain had done it.

There were many Americans who wanted to see Cuba gain her freedom from Spain. Some hoped that Cuba might, if independent, be annexed by the United States. William Randolph Hearst, whose newspaper the *Journal* had a wide circulation, did everything he could to stir up war wih Spain. He printed articles and cartoons—including false atrocity stories—to make the American public angry enough to fight. Hearst's rival publisher Joseph Pulitzer did the same thing in his *World.* The people who wanted war won out.

On April 19, 1898, Congress recognized Cuba as an independent nation. On April 20, diplomatic relations between the United States and Spain were cut off; and on April 21, President William McKinley asked Congress to declare war.

When the President declared war,

WILLIAM R. HEARST
THE YELLOW KID

Cartoons like this one of an angry Uncle Sam (left) helped rouse the United States to war. One of the patches on his back refers to the Maine, *the other to the death of a Cuban hero.*

The cartoon at right attacks the Journal *and Hearst for urging Americans to fight Spain.*

LOCATION OF THE MAINE-HAVANA HARBOR

ADMIRAL SICARD

The mysterious explosion of the battleship Maine *at Havana, on February 15, 1898, cost 260*

RECOVERING THE DEAD BODIES.

oril, the United States went to war with Spain after declaring Cuba an independent nation.

Commodore Dewey was in readiness with his small fleet at Hong Kong as Commander in Chief of the Asiatic Station (the United States naval forces in the Far East). Within ten days he was in enemy waters off the Spanish colony of the Philippines. As he arrived in enemy waters, Dewey could not help being concerned over the supply situation. While the Spanish would surely be aided by naval magazines at Cavite or Olangapo, the Americans were 7,000 miles away from their supply or repair base.

Commodore Dewey was aboard his flagship, the *Olympia*, of 5,870 tons. Though small compared with present-day ships, and poorly armored, she was classed as a "protected cruiser" and one of the finest in the Navy. Behind her in the darkness followed the lighter cruisers *Baltimore, Boston, Raleigh,* and *Concord*, and the 892-ton gunboat *Petrel*. In the convoy were also two supply steamers, *Nanshan* and *Zafiro*, escorted by the United States Coast Guard cutter *McCulloch*.

The night of April 30, 1898, was clear and calm in the South China Sea off Manila Bay and there was no sound in the placid waters save the throbbing of muffled engines and the steady swish of water along the sides of steel hulls. Outwardly, everything seemed peaceful as the six dark silhouettes that were Commodore George Dew-

On the bridge of the flagship U.S.S. Olympia stands Admiral George Dewey on the morning of May 1, 1898, at the Battle of Manila Bay.

ey's fighting ships moved toward their objective, Manila Bay. But to the Americans aboard this was a moment of strained suspense. Inside the harbor lay the warships of the Spanish Squadron, under Rear Admiral Don Patricio Montojo y Pasaron. And, covering at least four channels through which the American ships must pass, were heavy shore batteries.

As the *Olympia* approached the entrance to Boca Grande Channel at 11:00 P.M., a light shower briefly obscured the new moon. Yet it was still light enough for Dewey to make out the outlines of large Corregidor Island, as well as the smaller islands between which his ships would pass, Caballo and El Fraile.

Suddenly the lookout called, "Rockets to port!"

A signal had been fired from Corregidor. The American Squadron had been detected. The minutes passed in silence. No gunfire met them as they drew abreast of the two fortified islands. Was it because the waters were so heavily mined that the Spaniards considered it suicide for enemy ships to try to sneak through? The American Consul General at Singapore had informed Dewey four days earlier that the Boca Grande was heavily mined, and the Commodore had elected to run the risk.

Then, at twenty minutes past midnight, with the squadron halfway through the Channel, the stillness was broken by an abrupt "wharroom!" as the Spanish battery at El Fraile Island

105

opened fire. The *Olympia* was by this time too far beyond it to return the fire, but Dewey could hear the guns of his ships to the rear answering. The Spaniards fired only three shots and then, realizing that they could hardly see their targets, suddenly ceased fire.

At dawn the American Squadron stood directly off Manila. Now a few of the thirty-nine heavy guns of the city's battery began to open up on the intruders. Dewey calmly ignored them saving his own precious ammunition for the Spanish ships. He now steamed directly toward Admiral Montojo's squadron, which was lying to the southwest of Manila off the city of Cavite. As he approached, his officers could make out the Spanish line of battle formed by the flagship *Reina Cristina*, a cruiser of 3,520 tons, *Don Juan de Austria, Don Antonio de Ulloa, Isla de Luzon, Castilla, Isla de Cuba,* and *Marques del Duero.* Out of sight beyond were the *General Lezo,* the *Velasco,* and several small gunboats.

Commodore Dewey chose to attack in a battle column, with the *Olympia*

(under Captain C. V. Gridley) leading, followed by the *Baltimore, Raleigh, Petrel, Concord,* and *Boston.* As they closed for battle, the distance between ships was narrowed to two hundred yards in order that the fire might be concentrated more fiercely. The Spaniards, poorly trained in running battles, elected to wait at anchor, in order that the gunners would be able to take more careful aim.

It was 5:15 when the Spanish ships opened fire. By 5:35 the American guns were still silent. Then, when the

Olympia was less than 5,000 yards from the nearest Spanish ship, Commodore Dewey turned slowly to Captain Gridley standing next to him on the bridge and said calmly, "You may fire when you are ready, Gridley."

Dewey led his squadron westward, raking the immobile Spanish fleet with his port batteries; then swung about in a U-turn and cruised eastward, lashing the enemy with his starboard batteries. The American ships made a total of five runs.

When Admiral Montojo realized that his ships were being peppered like stationary targets, and that the fire of his gunners was pathetically ineffectual, he attempted to engage the enemy at closer quarters. Two of his ships, the *Austria* and *Cristina,* made heroic attempts to charge the American Squadron broadside as it passed. But he was hopelessly outclassed. The *Austria* and *Cristina* were met with such vicious fire that they were forced to turn back abruptly, with many casualties, both rapidly taking in water and both afire above decks.

But even as they limped away, Commodore Dewey was informed of a disheartening fact: the *Olympia* had used up all but fifteen rounds of ammunition for her five-inch guns. It was an anxious moment when Dewey said: "We will withdraw into the center bay." There he intended to redistribute am-

Spanish vessels Reina Cristina *and* Don Juan de Austria *receiving a final broadside from Admiral George Dewey's fleet on Manila Bay.*

munition amongst his ships and take stock of all casualties. It was a little before 8:00 A.M., less than two and a half hours after the battle had commenced.

As it turned out, the report to Dewey had been garbled in communication. The message should have told him that fifteen rounds of ammunition per gun had been *fired,* and not that this amount represented all that was left. Then Dewey discovered an incredible fact: as the captains arrived on board the flagship to report, it turned out that not a single life had been lost aboard the American ships, and only eight men had been slightly wounded. As for damage, the *Olympia* had been hit five times, one projectile having struck just under the bridge on which Dewey was standing; the *Baltimore* had been hit five times; and the *Boston,* four. The hits did little damage.

At 11:15 that morning, Dewey strode back onto the bridge and ordered his squadron back toward Cavite to continue the attack. What was his surprise to find that the only Spanish ship standing out to meet him was the dauntless *Don Antonio de Ulloa,* a small cruiser of only 1,160 tons. Behind her, as she set forth in a suicidal attempt to save face for the Spanish in the disastrous defeat, lay the smoking hulks of the remaining enemy ships. Admiral Montojo had lost 381 men killed or badly wounded out of his total complement of about 1,200.

When the *Ulloa* persisted in attacking and had been sunk by a few direct hits, the Spanish lowered their colors and flew white flags of defeat. The time was noon, on May 1, 1898.

The American public received the news with great satisfaction. Now, said the headlines in many papers, the *Maine* had been avenged.

If there were still any doubts after the Battle of Manila that American warships were far superior to those of the Spanish, they were quickly dispelled in the only other naval engagement of any import during the Spanish-American War. This was the one-sided Battle of Santiago.

The city of Santiago, near the southeastern end of Cuba, was the site of important land battles of the war, including the famous American charge up San Juan Hill. It had an important harbor, much used by the Spanish fleet. While Commodore George Dewey was fighting in Philippine waters, Rear Admiral William T. Sampson was blockading Cuban ports and bombarding shore batteries.

In an attempt to disrupt Sampson's destructive raids the Spanish Ministry of War dispatched a squadron from Spain under Admiral Pascual Cervera to patrol Cuban waters. Cervera arrived in the Caribbean around the middle of May, with no illusions whatsoever that his outclassed vessels could stand up to American units. After a clever game of hide-and-seek, in which he frustrated American intelligence agents completely, he slipped into the harbor at Santiago with his squadron on May 19. His situation was desperate. He badly needed

Signal flag from the
U.S.S. Olympia

The above picture shows the uniforms of United States
naval officers in 1899; from left to right, a Lieutenant,
Lieutenant Commander, Captain, Commander, Ensign,
and Naval Cadet. The poster below pictures enlisted
men aboard Dewey's flagship Olympia at Manila Bay.

1898 Navy Service Medal
for the Spanish Campaign

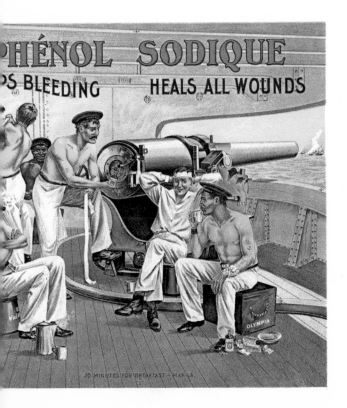

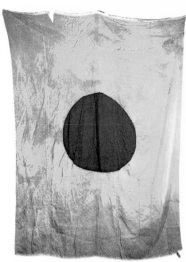

Signal flag from the
U.S.S. Olympia

coal; he could not count on ammunition supplies; and the long crossing from Spain had proven that his ships were ill-equipped for battle. Nevertheless, he did have one advantage: the harbor was well protected with a narrow entrance guarded by heavy gun emplacements. He would anchor his vessels inside and await developments.

On June 3, Admiral Sampson, fearing that the approaching hurricane season might drive his blockading ships away from the waters off the harbor entrance, decided to bottle up his opponent by sinking a vessel across the narrow mouth of the bay, only 100 yards wide. This inspired one of the really heroic actions of the war, when Mr. Richmond P. Hobson, a naval engineer, volunteered, with a crew of seven, to undertake the job. Well before daylight on June 3, they navigated the ancient collier, *Merrimac*, into the channel, intending to return on a life raft after sinking the vessel.

Waiting nervously outside, Admiral Sampson heard the sound of gunfire and saw flashes in the night. When dawn broke there was no sign of his gallant volunteers. They had sunk the collier—but not in the position intended. The current had carried her, after her tiller was shot away, too far into the harbor. That afternoon, a small boat, bearing a flag of truce, was seen emerging from the harbor entrance. Aboard was Admiral Cervera's Chief of Staff, to inform Sampson that his men had been rescued and were being held and accorded fair treatment by him as prisoners of war.

On June 6, the American fleet was to make its first attack on Santiago, causing light casualties on both sides. This was followed by a second inconclusive attack on June 16, after which little was to happen until July 3.

On land, the Americans had pushed their way up San Juan Hill, overlooking the city, after a bloody battle which took a heavy toll on both sides. It was then that General William R. Shafter, after sending a depressing message to Washington that his position was exceedingly precarious, decided that the best strategy was to bluff. He delivered an ultimatum to the Spanish commander, General José Toral, threatening to bombard the city unless he surrendered.

Hearing of this, Admiral Cervera decided to hurl his squadron at the Americans in what he knew would be a suicidal gesture. He quickly weighed anchor and headed directly for the harbor mouth in his flagship, the *Maria Teresa*. Behind her charged the *Vizcaya,* the *Cristobal Colon,* the *Almirante Oquendo,* and two torpedo-boat destroyers, the *Pluton* and *Furor.*

Cervera's desperate gesture was made because, as he had said before the battle, "If we should lose the squadron without fighting, the moral effect would be terrible, both in Spain and abroad." The Admiral had one slight hope. If he could ram the Amer-

In the great American victory at Santiago de Cuba, on July 3, 1898, Spanish Admiral Cervera's fleet of six ships was utterly destroyed.

ican fast cruiser *Brooklyn*, outside the harbor, with the *Teresa*, the others might escape from the slow battleships *Texas, Oregon, Iowa, Indiana*, and the armored cruiser *New York*.

His plan *almost* worked. Despite the astounding formality on the part of the Spanish of stopping at the harbor mouth to discharge the civilian pilots, the squadron actually managed to elude the astonished Americans and head westward. But the escape was short-lived. Having wooden decks, the Spanish ships were set afire one by one and forced to beach themselves in order to save what remained of their crews. That was virtually the end of the Spanish Navy. It was a costly defeat, for Cervera lost 323 of his men killed in action and 151 wounded. The Americans had one wounded and only a single death in one of the most lopsided battles in naval history.

The Spanish-American War marked the end of Spain's once great colonial empire in the New World. At its close America owned not only Puerto Rico but, through possession of Guam and the Philippines, a much larger share of control in the Pacific.

U-Boats and
Submarine Chasers

By the turn of the century, the American Navy had gained far more strength and experience than was indicated by the size and scope of the battles it had fought in the Spanish-American War. A significant change was taking place, too, in naval technology. The old style battleships, the *Monitor*-types and the rams, had become outmoded, and the coming vessel of war was the new type of battleship, known as the dreadnought. She was to have far heavier guns, as well as a range of sizes and types to make her able to meet a wider variety of battle situations. Then, too, there was an entirely new type of vessel, which had been developing as stealthily and unnoticed as she was to navigate later in time of war: the submarine. Ever since the days of the ill-fated *Hunley*, men had been perfecting submarines, and on October 12, 1900, a significant event took place with little fanfare or publicity. On that day, the SS-1, commonly known as the *Holland* (after her designer and builder, John Holland), became the first submarine commissioned by the

In the Straits of Magellan, at right, are the sixteen warships Theodore Roosevelt sent on the first round-the-world cruise of the United States Navy. They visited twenty nations and (for Japan's especial benefit) proved that America's fleet was second only to Britain's.

American Navy. Her first skipper was Lt. H. H. Caldwell, and for many an old-line naval officer, the assignment was looked upon as a dubious honor.

When Theodore Roosevelt took office as President in 1901, his policy was not only to spread good will abroad, but also to display the "Big Stick," as he termed military strength, so that no foreign nation would get the idea that

America could be easily bullied. He played a considerable part in pushing authorization for ten new battleships and four cruisers, as well as numerous smaller vessels. And during the eight years he was in office, the Navy increased from 25,000 enlisted personnel in 1900 to 45,000 in 1909.

Theodore Roosevelt's era is known, too, for the cruise of "The Great White Fleet" around the world during the years 1907-1909. American warships, painted white, and symbolic of peace, visited strategic foreign ports. Roosevelt felt that American diplomacy abroad would be more effective with a display of tonnage to give it weight.

Despite this expansion of the Navy, there were a number of shortcomings in equipment, personnel, and training when World War I began in 1914. When the United States entered the war in 1917, there were not enough ships prepared to combat what had, unexpectedly, turned out to be the greatest menace of all: the German U-boat. The 67 destroyers which the American Navy did have were effective against the U-boats but many more were needed—and were built before the war was over.

The shocking news of German submarine attacks on shipping in the vital Atlantic lanes was first learned by

America when Rear Admiral William S. Sims went to England at the start of the war to consult with the British Admiralty on joint naval matters. He learned that almost one-fourth of British shipping had already been sunk, that losses for April would amount to almost 900,000 tons; and that Germany would win the war in a matter of months if U-boat operations could not be curtailed. England could not exist on war matériel and food produced only within her own borders.

A few American ships were quickly readied for overseas duty. On May 4, 1917, six United States Navy destroyers arrived at Queenstown (Cobh), Ireland, under Commander Taussig. When the British Admiral in Ireland asked Taussig when the Americans could be prepared for action, he was astonished to hear, "We shall be ready when fueled."

No one knew it then, but the prompt action of the American Navy was to save the Allies at one of the most crucial moments in the war. By July 5, thirty-four American destroyers had arrived at Queenstown and Admiral Sims was advocating their use for convoying merchant ships. But there was opposition to his plan. "We cannot hold formation properly," said merchant ship captains, "we will have collisions at night, what with no running lights permitted. And the U-boats will torpedo us anyway."

Sims remained stubborn, and the Navy Department agreed to make a test. On June 14, a large convoy started on an historic voyage from New York across U-boat infested waters. It was divided into four groups. As the convoy neared Europe, destroyers from Queenstown steamed out to provide additional protection. Despite the detection of several marauding U-boats, one of which was damaged by a destroyer, not a ship received any injury. The convoy system had proven itself. From then on, U-boat commanders found that their field day was over. Their sinkings dwindled to about one-third of the former amount. And they were beginning to pay a price for their attacks, as American destroyers inflicted more and more damage. Then, on November 17, 1917, came the first big American victory. On that day, the U.S.S. *Fanning* sighted a periscope.

"Prepare to attack," ordered her skipper, Lieutenant Carpender.

At the same time, the nearby destroyer U.S.S. *Nicholson* was also alerted and both ships began depth charging. The periscope disappeared. The Americans did not know it, but 200 feet down the submarine *U-58* lay in hiding, trying to survive the depth charging from which she could not escape. Then her captain discovered that the explosions had wrecked the diving planes and broken oil lines. Rather than face certain destruction, the ship elected to surface and face

Before the United States entered World War I, the British liner Lusitania *was sunk by a German U-boat, May 7, 1915, off the Irish coast.*

114

capture. Moments later the captain and crew had been taken. But the U-boat, her sea cocks opened, sank before the Americans could board her and prevent the last-minute scuttling.

Though destroyers spearheaded America's naval attack, they were by no means the only vessels to see active service. Just as had happened in every major conflict in American history, World War I saw the emergence of new, improved types of naval vessels, armament, and equipment. Notable, of course, was the submarine. But many people overlook a unique American antidote to U-boats: the submarine chaser. Developed to complement the destroyer, this craft was slightly over one hundred feet long, armed with depth charges and three-inch deck guns. America built some 400 of these fast, efficient ships, known as the "splinter fleet" because they were small and made of wood.

Their first assignment, in the spring of 1918, was a gigantic blockading operation. The Allies (England, France, Italy, and the United States) had strung a 35-mile-long barrier of ships, mines, and balloons across the lower end of the Adriatic to bottle up Austrian submarines sneaking southward to raid the Mediterranean. Though the sub chasers were only part of the team, it is interesting to note that within two weeks after their arrival, enemy U-boat

the News That's Fit to Print."

The New York Times.

THE WEATHER
Fair today and Sunday, 'ress, to strong southwest to west win $_{ds}$,
☞For full weather report see Page 2.

NO. 20,923.   NEW YORK, SATURDAY, MAY 8, 1915.—TWENTY-FOUR PAGES.   ONE CENT In Greater New York, Jersey City and Newark.

TANIA SUNK BY A SUBMARINE, PROBABLY 1,000 DEAD;
ICE TORPEDOED OFF IRISH COAST; SINKS IN 15 MINUTES;
MERICANS ABOARD INCLUDED VANDERBILT AND FROHMAN;
WASHINGTON BELIEVES THAT A GRAVE CRISIS IS AT HAN

PRESIDENT
eply Stir-
ter and
isis.

TE HOUSE

m Closely,
on the
rse.

ESS CALL

ecalls Firm
; Warn-
any.

RUMORS

s to be Sunk
s Actual

a Times.
 T.—Never
ee years ago,
o Titanic had
gion been so
ver the stink.
The early re-
been no loss
at these ad-
o the greatest
when it be-
ad been many
are profound-
les that this
ce of Amer-
o bring about
onal relations

the sinking

The Lost Cunard Steamship Lusitania
X Where the First Torpedo Struck.   XX Where the Second Torpedo Struck.

SOME DEAD TAKEN ASHO

Several Hundred Surv
ors at Queenstown
and Kinsale.

STEWARD TELLS OF DISAS

One Torpedo Crashes Into
Doomed Liner's Bow, Anoth
Into the Engine Room.

SHIP LISTS OVER TO PO

Makes It Impossible to Lov
Many Boats, So Hundred
Must Have Gone Down.

ATTACKED IN BROAD D

Passengers at Luncheon—Warn
Had Been Given by Germans B
fore the Ship Left New York.

LONDON, Saturday, May
—The Cunard liner Lusitan
which sailed out of New Yo
last Saturday with 1,918 sou
aboard, lies at the bottom
the ocean off the Irish coast.
She was sunk by a Germa
submarine, which sent two to
pedoes crashed into her side
2:30 o'clock yesterday afte
noon while the passenge
seemingly confident that t
great, swift vessel could elu
the German underwater cra
were having luncheon.
The great inrush of wate
caused the liner to list hea

Cunard Office Here Besieged for News;
Fate of 1,918 on Lusitania Long in Doubt

Fate of Most of the Well-Known Passengers Still in Doubt
—Story of Disaster Long Unconfirmed While

Roosevelt Calls It Piracy;
Says That We Must Act.
Special to The New York Times.
SYRACUSE, N. Y., May
7—Ex-President Roosevelt

Meagre List of Saved,
Received in New York

Those whose rescue was
reported to New York by

Loss of the Lusitania Fills London
With Horror and Utter Amazement

News Held Back for Hours—Anxious Crowds Wait All
Night at Steamship Offices for Word of

INVEST IN 1
VICTORY LIBERT

activity there came to a standstill.

The American coast was subjected to very little raiding by U-boats. Submarines were not equipped for long stays in unfriendly waters where it was impossible to get fuel and food. Nevertheless, six sturdy boats did manage to cross the Atlantic with the intention of terrorizing the United States, and thus forcing the American

Navy to reassign many ships to home waters. The German plan failed, though some damage was done. The *U-151* shelled some small schooners off Cape Charles, then went on to sink 59,000 tons of shipping during a three-month patrol. The *U-156* sank a tug and four barges off Cape Cod and laid mines off Long Island. And the *U-140* sank a tanker, the *O. B. Jennings*, the

116

EY KEPT THE
SEA LANES
OPEN

L.A.SHAFER

OAN

ALL TOGETHER!

Enlist in the NAVY

The poster at left, urging citizens to buy government bonds, pictures a camouflaged American destroyer capturing a German U-boat. The other poster shows sailors of each of the Allied nations—Japan, France, the United States, Britain, Imperial Russia, and Italy—in common cause against Germany.

steamer *Merak,* and the Diamond Shoals lightship. The greatest German victory in American waters was the sinking of the cruiser *San Diego,* which struck a mine planted by an enemy U-boat off Fire Island on July 19, 1918. Though she sank within minutes, only six men were lost.

U-boats also tried to concentrate on supply and troop transports. The first two American transports to be torpedoed were the *Antilles* and the *Finland,* both in October, 1917. The large liner *President Lincoln* was another victim when, on May 31, 1918, while returning to the United States without escort, she was spotted by the *U-90* and sunk. Only twenty-six lives were lost—in direct contrast to the greatest disaster of all for the American Navy

117

during World War I, the sinking of the *Ticonderoga*.

Eight days out of New York, only a little more than a month before the end of the war, the cargo vessel found herself in difficulty. She could not keep up with her convoy and during the night of September 30, 1918, found herself dropping farther and farther behind. At dawn the lookout shouted.

"Submarine! Dead ahead!"

Commander J. J. Madison of the *Ticonderoga* made a split second decision. "Ram her!" he ordered, "All engines, flank speed!"

The distance closed fast, but the lumbering cargo vessel was not up to it. The German submarine *U-152* slid easily out of reach. Madison ordered his gun crew immediately into action. For two hours, the ships exchanged gunfire, but it was a lopsided fight. The U-boat could bombard the cargo ship broadside, while presenting only a tiny target herself, and her shells struck with devastating effect. Captain Madison was one of the first to be wounded, but he remained at his post.

Finally it was all over, the *Ticonderoga's* last gun blasted out of action. She was leaking badly from shell holes in her hull. The decks were smeared with blood and charred by fire.

"Abandon ship," gasped Madison, by this time barely conscious.

Even as the survivors scrambled exhaustedly aboard battered life rafts, the *Ticonderoga* sank beneath the waves. At a distance, despite pleas for medical aid, the *U-152* sat until certain her target was gone for good. Then the U-boat closed hatches and slid into

On November 17, 1917 (above) the destroyers Fanning *and* Nicholson *made the first American capture of a German sub—the U-58. Another surrenders in 1918 (below, left) and (right) a destroyer torpedoes an enemy sub.*

the deep to seek another victim. Of the 237 men aboard the American ship, only fourteen soldiers and ten seamen survived.

World War I was virtually over. Within a month, Austria was accepting truce terms and Germany was ready to collapse. With the signing of the Armistice on November 11, 1918, the great conflict came to an end. England, France, Italy, and the United States had joined forces on the land, at sea, and in the air, and had defeated a common enemy, the Central Powers.

Smashing the Axis Powers

Right after World War I, the Navy found itself occupied with a multitude of assignments necessitated by the state of a troubled and unsettled world. There were mine fields to remove, loose mines and hazardous wreckage to locate, displaced war refugees to be evacuated, and American lives to be protected in areas disrupted by civil strife. Then, too, there was the usual planning for the future.

In the spring of 1919, a handful of naval officers visualized a project that was to turn out to have world-wide significance. During World War I construction had been started on four transoceanic flying boats, but the aircraft had been completed too late to engage in actual maneuvers. These were Curtiss flying boats—airplanes with the designation "NC," often called "Nancys." A daring plan was proposed: why not test this new arm of the fleet by sending several of the planes across the Atlantic?

On May 8, three of the giant planes left the Naval Air Station at Rockaway, Long Island. The NC-3 was the flagship, followed by the NC-1 and the NC-4. Their destination was Newfoundland, from whence they were to fly to the Azores, off the coast of Portugal, then to Lisbon, and finally to Plymouth, England. The NC-4 proceeded no farther than Cape Cod before she had engine trouble and was forced to land for repairs. However, all three planes finally reached Newfoundland and on May 16, after refueling, headed out over the Atlantic for the long 1,380-mile hop to the Azores.

The NC-3 and the NC-1 were destined to fail just short of the goal. The NC-3 made a forced landing, and after fifty-three hours adrift on rough waters, managed to reach the port of Ponta Delgada in the Azores. The NC-1 was not so lucky. Down in open water, she took a heavy beating from the seas and began to sink. Only at the last moment was she sighted by the steamer *Ionia* and her crew rescued. But the NC-4, under the command of Lt. Commander Albert C. Read, flew on to Plymouth, England, to climax an achievement as significant as that of the *Mayflower*, which had set out from that very port three centuries before.

Naval insignia, decorations and campaign ribbons on the opposite page include: 1, the official United States Navy seal; 2, the Congressional Medal of Honor; 3, the Distinguished Flying Cross; 4, the Distinguished Service Medal; 5, Navy Commendation Medal; 6, Silver Star for gallantry in action; 7, Legion of Merit; 8, Navy Cross. The campaign ribbons signify: 9, World War II Victory; 10, service in the European-African-Middle East area; 11, a Presidential Unit Citation; 12, service in the Asiatic-Pacific area. Ribbons 13 and 14 were awarded by the government of the Philippines for Philippine Defense and Philippine Liberation, respectively.

The triumph of the *NC-4* was to have far-reaching results many years later, even though the era of the twenties was to see the Navy go into a decline with the scrapping of many ships under the disarmament policies of the time. Then, in the thirties, President Franklin Delano Roosevelt displayed much of the same interest in the Navy shown by an earlier Roosevelt—"Teddy." Alarmed at the rapid growth of the Axis powers—Germany, Italy, and Japan—in military strength, he helped to lay plans for increasing America's naval power and air strength.

But even the most farsighted American leaders had not counted on the viciousness of the enemy-to-be. High naval officers knew that trouble was in the wind. Throughout the Pacific, intelligence reports showed that the Japanese were establishing new bases and transporting troops to strategic points. It was expected, however, that the first outbreak of war would take place in the Far East.

Then came the quiet Sunday morning of December 7, 1941.

At a few minutes before 8:00 that morning, on the island of Oahu in the Hawaiian Islands, naval officers and men who happened to be out in the open began observing what seemed to be unusual air activity for such an early hour on a Sunday. They paused in what they were doing and stared

into the air before realizing that the planes did not look at all familiar.

In many places around the island men watched the planes disappear beyond nearby hills, wondering what it was all about. But at Pearl Harbor, the Navy's largest base in the Pacific, the situation was different—tragically so. Observers saw the strange planes dive towards them, emitting bursts of machine-gun fire. Out in the harbor, over the many American ships berthed there, dozens of the planes screeched in low, releasing deadly black bombs from under their bellies.

Within seconds the morning was shattered with the ear-splitting explosions of bombs and torpedoes. Jets of flame and pillars of smoke appeared among the ships and docks and warehouses. After the first stunned minute, the first American warning went out over the air, at exactly 7:58 A.M.:

AIR RAID. PEARL HARBOR.
THIS IS NO DRILL!

December 7, 1941, has been called "the most disastrous day in the entire history of the United States Navy." Of 202 naval planes, eighty were destroyed and seventy disabled, most without ever getting off the ground.

This panoramic painting of the Pearl Harbor disaster shows the capsized minesweeper Oglala, *in the foreground, and the burning battleships* Maryland *and* Tennessee *at far right.*

But it was in the waters of Pearl Harbor that the Navy suffered most. Here were assembled some eighty-six vessels of many types, which formed the major strength of the U.S. Pacific Fleet Of these, eighteen were destroyed or severely damaged. In all, the Navy suffered—on this single infamous day —a greater loss of personnel than it had during all of the Spanish-American War and World War I combined! The count added up to 3,077 killed or missing, and 876 wounded.

Through a stroke of good fortune, all of the American airplane carriers happened to be at sea when the attack came and thus escaped damage. This flaw in the timing of the Japanese was to prove extremely costly to Emperor Hirohito's fleet in the months to come.

But for the moment, the Japanese Navy remained in supreme control. On December 11, the American outpost at Guam in the Mariana Islands was captured, and the enemy was already taking over the Philippines. Yet, in the midst of all these easy victories, the Japanese encountered a stubborn nut to crack when they attacked the tiny island of Wake, a vital American naval air station in the very middle of the Pacific. Wake had a garrison of less than 450 men under Marine Major James P. Devereaux, no ships, and only twelve planes. Yet the courageous garrison held out for two weeks before the Japanese Navy was able to land troops to overrun the half-starved Americans. Even so, American planes and guns accomplished the remarkable feat of destroying an enemy cruiser, three destroyers, a gunboat, a submarine, and more than a dozen planes.

The months to come were ones of grim determination for the American Navy, as the enemy gained greater and greater control of the Pacific. There were few moments of glory for

AVIATOR'S INSIGNIA

OFFICER'S CAP DEVICE

SUBMARINE INSIGNIA

CAPTAIN'S EAGLE

ADMIRAL S'STARS

COMMANDER'S OAK LEAF

SEAMAN

SEAMAN (WHITES)

NAVY PILOT

OFFIC

United States Navy uniforms and insignia.

the United States. One exception was the Battle of Macassar Straits—not a big battle, but one which at the time served to boost American morale. On January 23, 1942, four ancient "four-pipers" (old destroyers with four tall stacks) steamed into the Macassar Straits, along the east coast of Borneo. They were the *Ford, Pope, Parrott,* and *Paul Jones,* under Commander Paul H. Talbot, U.S.N. They were stalking a large Japanese convoy, reported to have upwards of forty ships. Skirting the enemy destroyer escort, Talbot managed to slip in close enough to unloose all the torpedoes carried by his four destroyers. Then, in the darkness, he boldly let loose with all deck guns, estimating correctly that the Japanese would be too confused to determine which ships were friendly and which were Americans. That night the Japanese lost four transports. Of the four American destroyers, only the

Ford was struck, with injury to four of her men.

In early 1942, the Japanese Navy could move almost at will in the western and southwestern Pacific waters as it captured bases in the Philippines and throughout Indonesia. The American forces were largely limited to "raiding." A typical example of the raid technique was the hit-and-run action of fleet units in the Marshall and Gilbert Islands. On the morning of February 1, 1942, two carrier task forces engaged in a simultaneous strike. Vice Admiral William F. Halsey led the carrier *Enterprise,* with three cruisers and six destroyers, against the small atolls of Kwajalein, Wotje, and Maloelap in the central Marshalls. And Rear Admiral Frank J. Fletcher commanded the second force, which consisted of the carrier *Yorktown,* with two cruisers and four destroyers, in a raid against Jaluit and Mili atolls in the southern

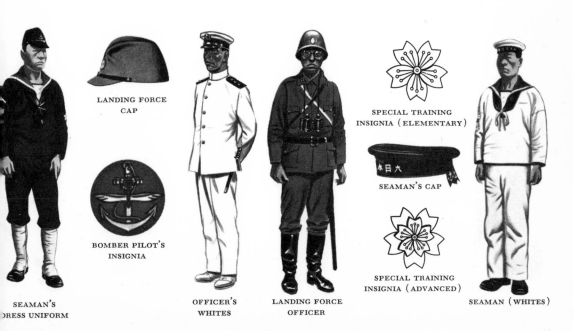

LANDING FORCE
CAP

BOMBER PILOT'S
INSIGNIA

OFFICER'S
WHITES

LANDING FORCE
OFFICER

SPECIAL TRAINING
INSIGNIA (ELEMENTARY)

大日本

SEAMAN'S CAP

SPECIAL TRAINING
INSIGNIA (ADVANCED)

SEAMAN (WHITES)

SEAMAN'S
DRESS UNIFORM

Imperial Japanese Navy uniforms and insignia.

Marshalls and against Makin in the northern Gilberts.

Small and spotty though American successes were, they rankled the Commander in Chief of the combined Japanese fleet, Admiral Yamamoto, the man who had conceived the infamous scheme of attacking Pearl Harbor. Now, he said, Japan must put an end to these irritating harassments by the American Navy, by taking over Mid-

way, just to the north of the Hawaiian Islands. Then he would force the U.S. fleet—weak from its losses at Pearl Harbor—to engage in a major battle somewhere near Hawaii.

There was one small detail which the Imperial Navy had to deal with first, however. To prevent the Americans from disrupting Japanese operations in the South Pacific, it would be wise to capture Port Moresby at the

lower end of New Guinea and establish a strong base. An invasion force was dispatched from Rabaul, with troop transports, cargo vessels, and tenders protected by three cruisers, two destroyers, and the small carrier *Shoho*. In addition, a powerful striking force was assembled to probe southward into the Coral Sea: two large airplane carriers, the *Shokaku* and the *Zuikaku,* as well as two cruisers, seven

destroyers, and a fuel tanker.

The time was late April, 1942. At that time the United States carrier, *Yorktown,* was patrolling the Coral Sea. And when it was learned by Allied intelligence agents that the Japanese were on the move southward, the carrier *Lexington* was ordered to join her. On May 5, the *Yorktown* rendezvoused with the *Lexington,* along with the following ships: an attack group of five cruisers and five destroyers; and a support group of three cruisers and two destroyers. Two other vessels, the tender *Neosho* and an escort, the destroyer *Sims,* were ordered south, away from the battle area.

It was not until May 7 that real action flared. At 10:00 A.M., an attack wave of ninety-two planes was launched from the *Yorktown* and the *Lexington,* and by 11:30 they had located the small Japanese carrier *Shoho* in the invasion force. American bombers made many hits; then the torpedo planes swooped in to finish the job and leave the enemy ship a sinking mass of twisted, smoking steel.

On that same morning, planes from the Japanese carrier force were far to the south, vainly seeking the American carriers. Suddenly, through a rift in the clouds that hung over the Coral Sea that day, they spotted the *Neosho* with her lone escort, the *Sims.* Ex-

On May 7, 1942, off Australia's northeastern coast during the Battle of the Coral Sea, 93 United States planes, including dive bombers, sank the Japanese aircraft carrier, Shoho.

The official navy photographs on this page show the destruction of the "Lady Lex," as the crew called the 33,000 ton American aircraft carrier Lexington. During the Battle of the Coral Sea, on May 8, 1942, the carrier managed to survive torpedo hits by Japanese planes. Several hours later, however, when gasoline vapor exploded between decks, the Lexington caught fire, and had to be abandoned. When she sank, 216 men were lost, but nearby destroyers saved 2,735 of the crew.

citedly, the Japanese pilots radioed that they had found the carriers. About seventy planes rushed to the area. Then, frustrated at finding nothing more, they unleased all their firepower on the two American ships. It was a hopeless battle. The *Sims* was all but obliterated. She broke completely in half and went down with a loss of all but thirteen of her officers and men. Somehow, miraculously, the *Neosho* managed to stay afloat, drifting for four days, before being located by an American destroyer, at which time her few survivors were picked up.

By 8:30 on the morning of May 8, each side had scouted out the other and knew its positions and strength. From the *Yorktown* and *Lexington*, 82 American planes took to the air, and from the *Shokaku* and *Zuikaku*, seventy planes. These flights passed each other somewhere en route to their targets, but too far away for sighting, and by 10:30 they were diving on their objectives. The American planes had little success. Intercepted by fast Zero Japanese fighters, they were able to make hits with only a few bombs and no torpedoes.

Meanwhile, the two American carriers were under heavy attack. To make matters worse, there were only seventeen Wildcat fighters to go aloft and intercept the enemy, along with sixteen bombers which attempted to serve as an anti-torpedo patrol. The *Yorktown* managed to avoid several torpedoes, and was given the bulk of the protection from the American escort ships. This turned out to be a serious error, for the *Lexington*, the larger of the two and the primary target, was quickly pounced upon. Two torpedoes struck her port side, along with three bombs. The resultant fires were extinguished, but nothing could be done about gasoline pipes which had been ruptured and were spewing gas and vapors throughout part of the ship. Suddenly, there came a tremendous explosion.

This was the end of the "Lex." After a futile all-day fight to control the fires, the order was given to abandon ship. And that night, Rear Admiral Frank J. Fletcher gave orders to a destroyer to torpedo and sink the flaming wreck of the carrier.

The Battle of the Coral Sea was the first great naval engagement in which the opposing ships remained completely out of sight of each other, an indication of the vital importance air power was to have in the future of the Navy. Victory or defeat? Despite the losses in ships (*Lexington, Neosho*, and *Sims*), in men (543), and in planes (66), the Americans had forced the Japanese to abandon the invasion of Port Moresby. And, even more important, they forced the enemy into making a decision that was to change the entire course of the war in the Pacific.

Admiral Yamamoto could wait no longer. He decided to make his prime move: to capture the American base at Midway and destroy the American fleet. He knew now, after the Battle of the Coral Sea, that much was in his favor: the *Yorktown* and *Lexington* were badly damaged—the latter, perhaps, sunk. The other big American carriers, the *Enterprise* and the *Hornet*, had been spotted in the South

Pacific, the Japanese thought, where they would undoubtedly remain for many weeks. And the only other carrier he need worry about, the *Saratoga*, was at Puget Sound, in the United States, undergoing repairs. Midway seemed to be Japan's for the asking.

The Japanese Admiral was well informed—on all matters but one: he could not guess that American intelligence officers were even then anticipating, from an examination of many scattered reports from scouting and reconnaissance units, that an attack on Midway would probably be made. Thus, while he was working out attack plans, urgent orders were going out to the *Enterprise* and *Hornet* to steam for Midway at top speed; for the *Yorktown* to proceed under forced draft to Pearl Harbor for rush repairs on her flight deck, damaged in the Battle of the Coral Sea; and for all available ships

to assemble at special rendezvous points. By the end of May, American forces for the protection of Midway consisted of eight cruisers, nineteen submarines (with others patrolling farther out), fourteen destroyers, the three carriers, and a small force of old battleships.

On May 28, 1942, the *Enterprise* and *Hornet*, with their escorts, sailed northwest under the command of Admiral Raymond A. Spruance, followed on May 30 by the refitted *Yorktown* and her escorts. Two days later the entire American force was consolidated into one unit under the command of Admiral Frank J. Fletcher. But, advancing on this defensive force from the northwest, west, and west southwest was one of the greatest enemy fleets ever assembled—more than one hundred ships, which included four powerful carriers, the *Kaga, Akagi, Hiryu,*

and *Soryu,* and eleven battleships, along with submarines, cruisers, destroyers, and other vessels. Following behind were cargo and transport vessels containing supplies and almost 4,000 invasion troops.

On June 3, at 9:00 A.M., a naval patrol plane spotted part of this great fleet some forty miles west southwest of Midway, and nine B-17 American bombers were dispatched from the Midway field to attack. On June 4, the battle began. Shortly after dawn, a large flight of enemy bombers approached Midway and began pounding shore installations.

The first American attack on the carrier force turned out to be a grim defeat. Army, Navy, and Marine

American dive bombers sink three Japanese carriers—the Akagi, Soryu, *and* Kaga—*in the furious Battle of Midway, on June 4, 1942.*

The photograph at far right shows the final plunge of the sinking destroyer Hammann, on June 4, 1942, at the Battle of Midway, after a direct hit from a Japanese submarine. The other three photographs, taken the same day, show the last moments of the huge aircraft carrier Yorktown, sunk in the same fight by Japanese torpedoes.

planes boldly attacked time after time, but the American losses were heavy and the Japanese remained unchecked. The second attack began when the carriers *Enterprise* and *Hornet* sent aloft more than one hundred planes to attack the enemy fleet. Suddenly, however, the Japanese changed course and caused great confusion among the American airmen, who found only open water where they expected to sight targets. Characteristic of American courage and audacity was the case of Torpedo Squadron 8. This was composed of eighteen planes from the *Hornet*, the first ones to reach the enemy, a little after 9:00 A.M. that day. Though the planes were almost out of gasoline, Lieutenant Commander John C. Waldron, the Squadron Leader, ordered his pilots to the attack. All eighteen were shot down, one by one. The lone survivor was Ensign George H. Gay, who found himself floundering undetected in mid-ocean, surrounded by the enemy ships, where he could watch the rest of the U.S. planes attack.

What he saw before being rescued was spectacular. Four bombs struck the *Kaga*, setting it afire from one end to the other. Two more struck the *Akagi*, and three the *Soryu*, leaving the ships burning and helpless. Only the *Hiryu* escaped undamaged. Later the American submarine *Nautilus* finished off the *Soryu* completely. The *Kaga* went down; and the *Akagi's* hulk was purposely torpedoed by the Japanese on June 5.

During World War II many islands of the South Pacific were dotted with naval bases, used to fuel and supply the ships and airplanes engaged in fighting the Japanese. One such typical base, at Espiritu Santo, in the New Hebrides Islands, is shown above. The night action, below, occurred on November 14, 1942, off Savo Island, near Guadalcanal, in the fiercely-contested Solomons group.

Around noon of June 4, forty Japanese fighters and dive bombers headed toward the *Yorktown* to avenge the disgrace. Though most were shot down, they managed to make three bomb hits on the carrier which caused severe damage. Firefighters had barely brought the blazes under control when a new attack began. All of the attackers were destroyed, but not before two managed to hit the *Yorktown* with torpedoes, both amidships. The great carrier was mortally wounded. The order was given to abandon ship, at 2:45 P.M.

Now the American planes concentrated on the carrier *Hiryu*, knowing that once she was sunk the enemy would be unable to launch further air attacks. Almost within a matter of minutes after being located on June 5, she was left afire from stem to stern, and was later scuttled. The final blow came on June 6, when bombers from *Hornet* and *Enterprise* sank the heavy cruiser *Mikuma*. The Americans, however, were to suffer one further loss, that of the destroyer *Hammann*. Hit by the Japanese submarine *I-168*, she sank with one-third of her crew, while attempting to put a salvage party aboard the listing *Yorktown*. The carrier went down finally in the same attack. The Americans had won a great victory, destroying four carriers, two heavy cruisers, four destroyers, and 300 planes. This was the first decisive defeat suffered by the Japanese Navy in 350 years!

From the very beginning of World War II, most of the actions of the United States Navy were fought in the Pacific, against the Japanese, rather than in Atlantic waters against the Axis powers of Europe. There were, of course, notable exceptions. German submarine threats to Atlantic shipping, particularly in the early years of the war, made it necessary for the United States Navy to carry on a long, dangerous campaign of anti-submarine warfare. In October, 1942, the Navy was called upon to help support the combined landings of the Allies in North Africa, with a special "Western Task Force" that included the carrier *Ranger,* four escort carriers, three battleships, seven cruisers, and a flotilla of destroyers and other supporting ships. In July, 1943, a similar task force was formed, and helped to make possible the Allied invasion of Sicily, just off the southern tip of Italy. And, then, in the winter and spring of 1944, the Navy continued its support of landing operations—such as the bitter battle for the Anzio beachhead—all up and down the Italian coast.

On D Day, June 6, 1944, the Allies launched their invasion of German-occupied France. This invasion, which took place on the Normandy coast, was made possible by the largest fleet or armada ever assembled for a war—4,000 American, British, Canadian, French, Dutch, and Norwegian ships. The armada—which was based in several English ports—carried troops, supplies, and ammunition to the French coast. It also included ships to

ALLIANCE
(Frigate—1778)

CONSTITUTION
(Frigate—1798)

FULTON
(Experimental
Steam Sloop—1815)

MISSISSIPPI
(Steam Sloop—1841)

BOSTON
(Protected Cruiser—1886)

CUSHING
(Torpedo Boat—1890)

INDIANA
(Battleship—1896)

WIC
(Destroy

BALLAO
(Submarine—1941)

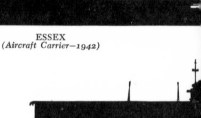

ESSEX
(Aircraft Carrier—1942)

IOWA
(Battleship—1944)

FORREST
(Aircraft Carrie

attack and destroy German submarines attempting to halt the invasion and ships which could bombard German coastal installations.

Meanwhile, out in the far Pacific, an entirely different type of warfare was being waged. In the summer of 1942, not long after the Battle of Midway, the Americans were struggling to establish bases in the hot and fever-ridden jungles of the Solomon Islands.

For the Navy, it was a time of grim, seesaw struggle for survival. After a disastrous defeat at Savo Island, in which 2,000 American lives were lost, the Navy bounced back in the Battle for the Eastern Solomons, sinking a carrier and two other vessels. This was followed by the Battle of Cape Esperance on October 11 and 12, 1942, during which both sides took considerable punishment, and by the Battle of the Santa Cruz Islands two weeks later, during which the American Navy suffered heavy losses.

On November 12 and 13, the American Navy was to make a supreme sacrifice in men and ships in the Battle of Guadalcanal, off the Solomon Islands. Yet, in so doing, the Navy was to help the Marines and the Army establish a strong enough footing on Guadalcanal so that the enemy was never thereafter to recapture the island. While the seesaw battle on land was still in the balance, five American cruisers and eight

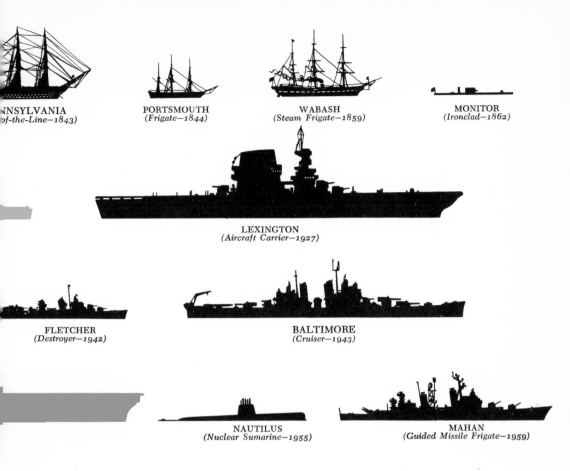

PENNSYLVANIA
(Ship-of-the-Line—1843)

PORTSMOUTH
(Frigate—1844)

WABASH
(Steam Frigate—1859)

MONITOR
(Ironclad—1862)

LEXINGTON
(Aircraft Carrier—1927)

FLETCHER
(Destroyer—1942)

BALTIMORE
(Cruiser—1943)

NAUTILUS
(Nuclear Sumarine—1955)

MAHAN
(Guided Missile Frigate—1959)

The growth in power of the United States Navy is seen in these silhouettes, made to scale, of famous classes of ships. Note also the transition from sail to steam.

destroyers, under the command of Rear Admiral Daniel J. Callaghan, were ordered to skirt the north coast of Guadalcanal to protect troop transports and intercept expected units of the enemy. Heading toward the American ships, on the night of November 12, was a strong Japanese force determined to break up all attempts the Americans made at landing.

Shortly after midnight, the two forces had detected each other, and by 1:30 A.M. were about to engage in one of the most confused battles of the war. With radar difficulties hindering both

sides, the opposing ships had to rely on visual contact and the use of searchlights. It became a wild duel between individual ships. The American flagship *San Francisco* was hit numerous times around 2:00 A.M., during which action Admiral Callaghan and most of his staff were killed. The battle lasted less than half an hour, after which both sides retreated in disorder. Two American destroyers had been sunk;

OVERLEAF: *The Battle of the Santa Cruz Islands was fought southeast of Guadalcanal on October 26, 1942. Here Japanese aircraft are attacking an American battleship and carrier.*

137

DWIGHT SHEPLER
USNR
'21

two more were sinking; the cruiser *Atlanta* was so gutted by explosions she had to be sunk; all other ships except one were badly damaged. And as a finale, the cruiser *Juneau*, as she retired, was torpedoed by a submarine, broke in two, and went down with all but ten of her crew of nearly seven hundred.

Throughout November and December the Americans and Japanese met in battle several more times before Guadalcanal was finally secured. The United States lost a total of twenty-four large ships to nineteen for the enemy. But the Americans achieved a victory, in wresting control of the islands, which marked a turning point in the war in the Pacific.

While the U.S. Navy in the South Pacific sweltered under the tropical sun, other units fought the stinging cold and everlasting fog of the Arctic to establish bases in the thin necklace of rocky islands stretching westward from Alaska, known as the Aleutians. Early in 1943, the Japanese decided to wipe out the bases built by the Americans near their own holdings at Attu and Kiska. In March, the Japanese dispatched a convoy, with troops and supplies, to Attu, escorted by two heavy cruisers, two light cruisers, and four destroyers. Getting word of this,

Rear Admiral Charles H. McMorris boldly sped to intercept the force with a smaller group, consisting of one heavy cruiser, one light cruiser, and four destroyers. Suddenly the Admiral realized that he was greatly outnumbered in heavy guns, but it was too late for retreat because the enemy was now between him and his home port. Nevertheless, he managed to inflict so much damage on the enemy that they finally withdrew without a victory.

The American ships were hit again

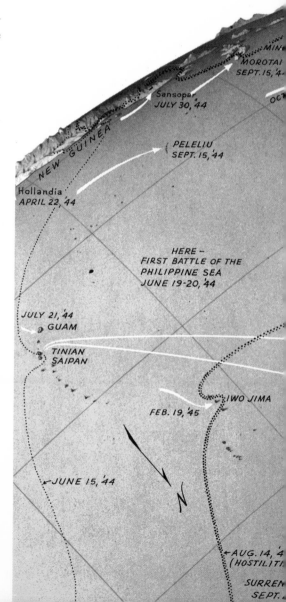

This map, which looks southwest over the Pacific, illustrates the scope of the "island-hopping" campaigns that sent American forces to the Philippines, Iwo Jima, and Okinawa, and brought about final victory over Japan.

m left to right,
RICAN ADMIRALS:

LIAM F. HALSEY
RLES H. MC MORRIS
EST J. KING
MAS C. KINKAID

RC A. MITSCHER
STER W. NIMITZ
IEL J. CALLAGHAN
MOND A. SPRUANCE

The U.S.S. Emmons *is shown aiding the massive invasion of Normandy on D-Day, June 6, 1944. This sector of Omaha beach, at Colleville-sur-Mer, was called Fox Green Beach.*

and again, especially the heavy cruiser U.S.S. *Salt Lake City*. But all managed to return to their base, despite the lopsided battle, having so discouraged the enemy that he decided against trying to reinforce his Aleutian bases. And in the spring of 1943, the Americans occupied Attu and later forced the evacuation of Kiska.

By early 1944, United States forces were on the move westward, pushing the enemy off one island in the Pacific after another. The Gilbert Islands had been taken, then the Marshalls. And by June 15, 1944, American troops were already landing on the large island of Saipan, in the Marianas, heavily supported by naval units under the command of Admiral Spruance. On June 16—the morning after D-Day at Saipan—Spruance learned that main units of the Japanese fleet had sortied through San Bernardino Strait and into the Philippine Sea. This was to be the Battle of the Philippine Sea.

On June 19, the Japanese had approached close enough to Saipan to launch heavy air strikes against the American troops and ships concentrated along the shore. But the U.S. Navy was striking back. On that same day the submarines *Albacore* and *Cavalla* sank the *Taiho* and *Shokaku*—two of the enemy's largest carriers.

This was to be an eventful day. At 10:00 that morning, Admiral Marc

Mitscher's Fast Carrier Force (part of Spruance's fleet) made contact with large numbers of Japanese planes approaching from the west. All day long, American pilots took off from the carrier decks in relays, pouncing upon the enemy with such skill and speed that, by dusk, they had chalked up such an incredible score that it has ever since been referred to as "The Marianas Turkey Shoot." Against relatively small American losses of only twenty-six planes, the enemy lost

a grand total of 402 of their aircraft.

Following through on this unique victory, Admiral Spruance now ordered Mitscher's Fast Carrier Force to pursue the enemy carriers that had launched the ill-fated Japanese planes. All that night Mitscher headed west at full speed. Not until the middle of the afternoon of June 20 were the Japanese ships located. Mitscher immediately ordered twenty-one planes into the air, knowing the enemy lay almost at the end of their range. By 6:20 P.M., the American planes were over their targets, where they knocked down twenty of the pitifully small force of thirty-five opposing planes that remained, sank one carrier and two fleet oilers, and damaged four other carriers, one battleship, a cruiser, and an oiler.

Although twenty American planes were lost in combat, and eighty more went down in the water, out of fuel on the long return flight, only thirty-eight fliers were killed or missing.

143

INVASION of LEYTE, P.I. SHOWING PART

This tremendous loss of air power by the Japanese was a key factor in the subsequent seizure by American forces of Guam and Tinian, the other major islands in the Marianas. And by the end of the summer, the Japanese knew that the Americans were now close enough, and strong enough, to prepare to recapture the Philippines. The situation reached its crisis in the Battle of Leyte Gulf.

It was in October, 1944, that the U.S. Navy organized its strength in the Philippines to assist General Mac-Arthur's landings on the island of Leyte in the Philippines.

When the Japanese learned of the invasion plans, they hastily dispatched three fleets toward the Philippine Sea: the Second Fleet, with five battleships, twelve cruisers, and fourteen de-stroyers under Admiral Nishimura; the Third Fleet, which streamed south from Japanese waters, with four carriers, two carrier-battleships, two cruisers, and eight destroyers under Admiral Ozawa; and the Fifth Fleet, a small force of three cruisers and four destroyers which was then prowling off Formosa, under Admiral Shima.

Against this array of 61 major vessels, the U.S. Navy had a formidable array: the Seventh Fleet, under Admiral Kinkaid, which had three groups of four escort carriers each, plus six battleships and their support vessels; the Third Fleet, under Admiral Halsey, with six fast battleships, cruisers, destroyers, and four carrier groups. The Americans also had some 500 landing craft and transport vessels along the shore at Leyte—all of which

The sea is black with landing craft off Leyte Island, in the Philippines, as the American invasion, supported by Admiral Kinkaid's Seventh Fleet, begins on October 20, 1944. From October 24-25 was fought the Battle of Leyte Gulf.

had to be protected.

In the early dawn of October 23, two American submarines made the first contact, locating the Japanese Second Fleet. The *Darter* drew first blood, sinking the heavy cruiser *Atago,* later crippling another cruiser, the *Takao,* and putting her out of the battle. The second submarine, the *Dace,* sank another cruiser, the *Maya.* A day later, on October 24, planes from two of the American carrier groups had also located the Japanese Second Fleet. By dusk, they had damaged every battleship in the fleet, sunk a destroyer, and forced the heavy cruiser *Myoko* to limp homeward, out of action. But the biggest conquest was sinking one of the largest warships ever built, the 73,000-ton *Musashi.*

On that same day, Japanese pilots spotted units of the American Third Fleet, to the northeast of Leyte. Bombers from Japanese fields on the island of Luzon in the northern Philippines took off to attack. They were joined by planes from Admiral Ozawa's Third Fleet, whose four carriers were steaming at full speed down from the north. American pilots quickly rose to the attack, shooting down more than one hundred planes of the enemy. In return, however, the Japanese bombed the small carrier *Princeton* and set her afire. Shortly after she was abandoned, she blew up, killing 200 of the crew of the cruiser *Birmingham,* which had drawn alongside to pump water into

her flaming wreckage.

Now the Japanese tried a great trick. The Japanese Third Fleet did everything possible to attract attention: making heavy columns of smoke, breaking radio silence, and sending two ships south to be sighted. Admiral Ozawa's mission was a suicidal one. He was trying to attract the full brunt of the American strength in order to draw the U.S. fleets away from the Japanese Second Fleet, and from the small Japanese Fifth Fleet. In this way, the Admiral hoped that he could distract American forces long enough so the other Japanese ships could sneak into the Leyte area and halt the American invasion.

The trick was partially successful. Admiral Halsey now committed most of the strength of his Third Fleet to the north. This was an error, but no one could have realized this at the time, for the American believed that Admiral Ozawa had no less than eight carriers, instead of four, and that their decks were loaded with planes (in reality there were only seventy-six left). Halsey's Third Fleet attacked quickly and registered hits on all four carriers. The light carrier *Chitose* was sunk, along with a destroyer, and the big carrier *Zuikaku* was disabled so she could no longer steer properly. A light cruiser, the *Tama,* was put out of action. And soon afterward the *Zuikaku* was bombed until she sank.

While this action was going on, the Americans were in serious difficulty to the south, off Leyte. The largest Japanese force, the Second Fleet under Admiral Kurita, had been sighted heading to the west—steaming at full speed *away* from the Americans. However, as soon as Admiral Ozawa had used his Third Fleet to lure Admiral Halsey's Third Fleet to the north, the Japanese Second Fleet changed course abruptly and headed back *toward* Leyte. Admiral Shima's Japanese Fifth Fleet had also arrived for battle, to meet only the American Seventh Fleet under Admiral Kinkaid.

Early in the morning of October 25, two battleships, one cruiser, and four destroyers of the Japanese Second Fleet steamed up from the south and began battling two waiting squadrons of destroyers. The flagship *Yamashiro* (a battleship) went down. One Japanese destroyer followed and two others were so badly crippled that a little while later they were also sunk. The second of the two battleships, the *Fuso,* began to sink; and the heavy cruiser *Mogami* was last seen on fire and partially out of control.

At about the same time this action was taking place, Admiral Shima's Japanese Fifth Fleet was coming up from the south too. One cruiser, the *Abakuma,* was quickly put out of action by American PT boats. A second, the *Nachi,*was seriously damaged when she rammed the disabled *Mogami.* So Admiral Shima rallied what ships he had left and retreated to the south.

Now the main Japanese force, the Second Fleet, pounced down on Leyte from the north: four battleships, eight cruisers, and eleven destroyers. At 6:45 in the morning of October 25, it made contact with a smaller American force: six escort carriers, three destroyers, and four small destroyer escorts. The Americans hastily turned south to prevent complete annihilation, with the destroyers and destroyer escorts stabbing back heroically at the enemy as they ran. The *Johnston, Samuel B. Roberts,* and *Hoel* were sunk, however, and most of the other American ships severely damaged. The carrier *Gambier Bay* was pounded endlessly by Japanese shells until she sank. A little later the carrier *St. Lô* was struck by a bomb from a plane and sank.

Other American forces, in the form of torpedo planes and bombers, were arriving to help by this time, and Admiral Kurita, jubilant over his initial success, was given some of his own medicine as the heavy cruiser *Suzuya* was bombed to the bottom and two others, the *Chikuma* and *Chokai*, were rendered helpless in the water. At this point the Admiral decided to retreat.

Even in retreat he was not safe. The next day, planes from the American carrier groups went after the Japanese Second Fleet and polished off the light cruiser *Noshiro*. Thus ended the Battle of Leyte Gulf. In comparison with the six ships lost by the U.S. Navy during the battle, the Japanese had lost four aircraft carriers, three battleships, ten cruisers, and nine destroyers—more tonnage than had ever been sunk before in a single battle or in so brief a time. Pearl Harbor was avenged, and from that moment on, until the end of the war nine months later, the Japanese Navy was fighting a lost cause.

Throughout all the battles in the Pacific, one type of vessel emerged as the most effective single type in the entire United States fleet: *the submarine*. From Pearl Harbor on, until the end of the war in the Pacific in August, 1945, American submarines sank more tonnage than all other naval and air units combined. In all, American submarines accounted for 1,178 merchant ships and 214 major naval vessels. The biggest prize of all was that of the *Archerfish*, which dispatched a 59,000-ton Japanese aircraft carrier. Another submarine, the *Tang*, achieved the notable record of sinking 93,824 tons of Japanese shipping in only nine months; while another, the *Rasher*, rolled up a record of 99,901 tons in ten months.

This was an indication of the new type of naval warfare that was developing, and of the new tactics that would be needed in the future. Perhaps the most significant of all developments since World War II for the American Navy has been the perfection of the nuclear submarine, which can cruise for weeks under the ocean without once coming to the surface. Torpedoes are on the way out; in their place are the new types of missiles, which can be fired from hundreds of feet below the surface and directed thousands of miles to an enemy target.

True to its tradition, the United States Navy is continuing today, as it did in the days of the Revolution and the War of 1812, to back up the courage and determination of its officers and men by keeping one step ahead of enemies—both real and potential— with new developments. Throughout the history of the Navy, ingenuity and imagination have always gone hand-in-hand with the daring deeds and brave men who have met grave situations face to face and wrested victory from defeat.

World War II ended officially on September 2, 1945, when Japan signed an unconditional surrender aboard the battleship Missouri.

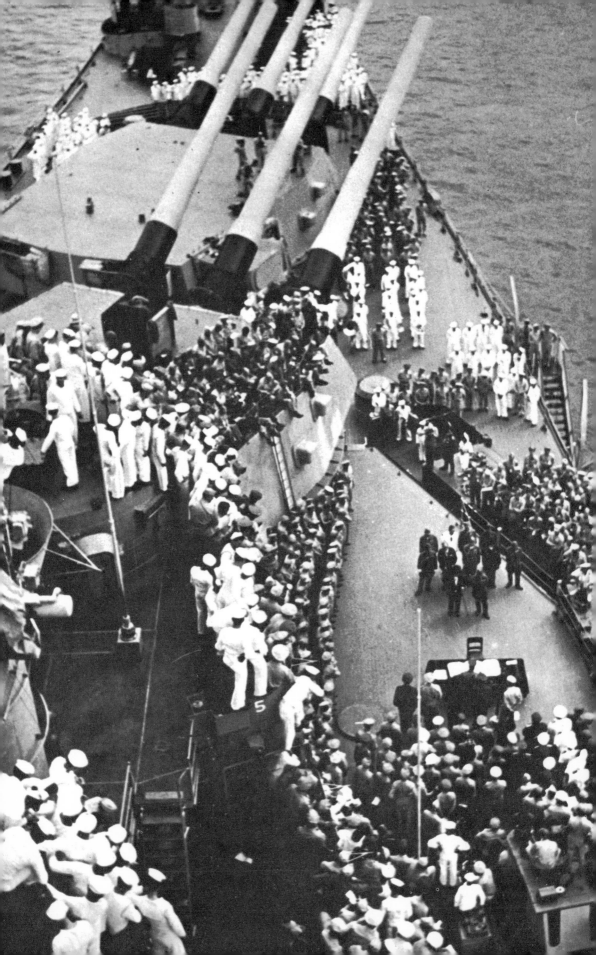

APPENDIX

AMERICAN HERITAGE PUBLISHING CO., INC. • BOOK DIVISION: Richard M. Ketchum, EDITOR. JUNIOR LIBRARY: Ferdinand N. Monjo, EDITOR, John Ratti, ASSISTANT EDITOR. Malabar Schleiter • Judy Sheftel • Julia B. Potts • Mary Leverty, EDITORIAL ASSISTANTS. DESIGN: Emma Landau.

PICTURE CREDITS

The source of each picture used in this book is listed below, by page. When two or more pictures appear on one page, they are separated by semicolons. The following abbreviations are used.

AH—American Heritage Collection
CHS—Chicago Historical Society
CAD-USND—Combat Art Div., U. S. Navy Department
FDRL—Franklin D. Roosevelt Library, Hyde Park, N. Y.
INHPC—Independence National Historical Park Collection
ISOC—Irving S. Olds Collection, New York City
LC—Library of Congress, Washington
MM—Mariners Museum, Newport News, Virginia
NA—National Archives, Washington

NYHS—New York Historical Society, New York City
NYPL—New York Public Library, New York City
NM—Norfolk Museum, Norfolk, Virginia
OUSNP—Official U. S. Navy Photographs
OPS—Old Print Shop, New York City
SI—Smithsonian Institution, Washington
USNAM—Courtesy U. S. Naval Academy Museum, Annapolis, Md.
USND—United States Navy Department

Cover: Painting by Thomas Birch, USNAM. Front end sheets: (top l.) Charles Willson Peale, INHPC; (bot. l. & r.) Rembrandt Peale, NYHS; (top r. & cen. l. bot.) USNAM; (cen. l. top) SI; (cen. & cen. r.) LC. Half title: FDRL. Title: Courtesy of Mr. Warren Sturgis. Contents: MM. 10 Flags (top l. & top r.) CHS; Flags (top cen., bot. l. & bot. r.) USNAM; Portrait (cen.) FDRL; Grapple, Anchor, & Rope, *Liber Nauticus*, Dominic and John Serres, London, 1805, NYPL; Sextant & Quadrant, LC. 12 (top to bot.) *The Kedge Anchor*, William N. Brady, 1903, NYPL; op. cit.; *The Kedge Anchor*, William N. Brady, 1857, MM; op. cit. 13 The Bailey Coll. MM. 14-15 Crown copyright reserved. Reproduced from the drawing in the Cumberland Papers, Royal Collection, Windsor Castle, by Gracious Permission of H. M. the Queen. 16 (top) *Liber Nauticus*, NYPL; (bot.) *Kedge Anchor*, 1863, MM. 16-17 op. cit. 17 op. cit. 18-19 Richard Paton, USNAM. 20 (l.) *Letters and Papers Relating to the Cruises of Gustavus Conyngham*, ed. Robert W. Neeser, NYPL; (r.) Peale, INHPC. 21 *Kedge Anchor*, 1863, MM. 22 (top) OPS; ISOC. 23 (top) Courtesy Mr. Arthur C. Bonnycastle; (bot.) SI. 25 (top) National Maritime Museum; (bot. l.) Gilbert Stuart, USND; (bot. r.) C. W. Peale, INHPC. 26 Louis Crepin, USNAM. 27 C. W. Peale, INHPC. 28-29 ISOC. 29 (top) Bass Otis, Long Island His. Soc. (bot.) Gilbert Stuart, USND, Permission Mr. James J. Ryan. 30-31 Steel, Vol. 1, 1794, MM. 32 NYHS. 33 (both) SI. 34-35 Atwater Kent Museum, Philadelphia. 36 (top) ISOC; (bot.) FDRL. 38-39 Michele Corné, USNAM. 40 (top) Gilbert Stuart, SI; (bot.) ISOC. 41 ISOC. 42 (top) FDRL; (bot.) ISOC. 43 ISOC. 44 Peabody Museum, Salem, Mass. 45 OPS. 46-47 Thomas Birch, USNAM. 49 ISOC. 50 (top to bot.) AH; ISOC; AH; AH; AH; AH. 50-51 NA. 52-53 Ambroise Louis Garneray, 1822. 54 *Greenwich Hospital, A Series of Naval Sketches Descriptive of the Life of a Man-of-War's Man, by An Old Sailor* (M. H. Barker), 1826, NYPL. 55 (all) FDRL. 56-57 OPS. 58-59 FDRL. 59 *Narrative of the United States Exploring Expedition*, Charles Wilkes, USN, Vol. 2, 1844, NYPL. 60 (top) MM; (bot.) Courtesy of the Metropolitan Museum of Art, Rogers Fund, 1941. 62 MM. 62-63 H. Walke, Lt. USN, USNAM. 64-65 FDRL. 66-67 (all) NM. 68 (top) Collection of DeWolf Perry; (bot.) LC. 68-69 FDRL. 70 Harper's Weekly, 1861, AH. Color by Delwin Cunningham. 72-73 NYHS. 73 (both) NA.

74-75 CHS. 76 Map drawn expressly for this book by John Teppich. 78 (top) Courtesy Julia B. Potts; (bot.) Map drawn expressly for this book by John Teppich. 79 (bot.) op. cit.; (top) MM. 80 NYHS. 80-81 *Battles and Leaders of the Civil War*, Vol. 1, 1884-1887, AH. 81 (top to bot.) Brown Brothers; op. cit.; NA; NYHS. 82 (top) OPS; (bot.) Collection of Oliver Jensen. 84 (top) NM; (bot.) LC. 85 LC. 86-87 FDRL. 88 (top to bot.) Leslie's Illustrated Newspaper, 1865, AH; NA; *Battles and Leaders*, Vol. 4, 1888, NYPL. 90-91 Louisiana His. Assoc. 90 (cen.) Conrad Wise Chapman, The Confederate Museum; (bot.) Submarine Library, General Dynamics Corp. 91 (top) op. cit.; (bot.) SI. 92 (l.) Cook Collection, Valentine Museum; (r.) The Bettmann Archive. 93 Collection of Sir Stanley Spurling, St. George, Bermuda. 94 (top) LC; (bot.) MM. 97 Map drawn expressly for this book by John Teppich. 98-99 NYHS. 100 *Leslie's Official History of the Spanish-American War*, NYPL. 101 *The Bee*, June 8, 1898, Vol. 1, NYPL. 102-103 CHS. 104 R. F. Zogbaum, Courtesy State of Vermont. 106-107 LC. 109 (top l.) Courtesy of Bennett Feldman; (top r.) USNAM; (cen.) NYHS; (bot. l.) LC; (bot. r.) USNAM. 111 FDRL. 112-113 Henry Reuterdahl, USNAM. 115 NYPL. 116-117 SI. 117 FDRL. 118 & 119 (all) LC. 120 (Seal & Medals) USND; (Ribbons) NYHS. 122-123 Griffith Bailey Coale, CAD-USND. 124 Drawn expressly for this book by Don Lynch. 125 U.S. Military Academy Library, West Point. 126-127 Robert Benny, CAD-USND. 128 & 129 OUSNP. 130-131 Coale, CAD-USND. 132 & 133 OUSNP. 134 (top) William F. Draper, CAD-USND; (bot.) Dwight C. Shepler, CAD-USND. 136-137 *Dictionary of American Naval Fighting Ships*, Vol. 1, 1959, USND. 138-139 Shepler, CAD-USND. 140-141 Courtesy of Richard Edes Harrison. 141 (all except Callahan) OUSNP; (Callaghan) USNAM. 142-143 Shepler, CAD-USND. 144-145 FDRL. 146 Draper, CAD-USND. 149 Wide World. Back End Sheet: (top l., cen. l., bot. l., & bot. r.) USNAM; (cen. top l., cen. top. r., top r., top r., & cen. r.) USND; (cen.) Dwight C. Shepler, CAD-USND; (cen. bot.) Courtesy John T. McCoy, Jr. Back Cover: (top to bot.) *"United States* and *Macedonian."* Thomas Birch. NYHS; Seahorse Tattoo, MM; Page from Commodore Truxton's Signal Book, USND; Cigar Store Sailor, NYHS; U.S. Naval Uniforms, 1812, NYHS.

FOR FURTHER READING

Young readers seeking further information on Naval Battles and Heroes will find the following books to be both helpful and entertaining:

American Heritage. *Famous American Ships*, ed. Walter Franklin. New York: Golden Press, 1958.

Durant, John and Alice. *Pictorial History of American Ships*. New York: A. S. Barnes & Co., 1953.

Hansen, Harry. *Old Ironsides, the Fighting Constitution*. New York: Random House, 1955.

Icenhower, Joseph B. *Submarine Rendezvous*. Philadelphia: Winston, 1957.

Kühn, Ferdinand. *Commodore Perry and the Opening of Japan*. New York: Random House, 1955.

Mitchell, Helen, and Wilson, W. N. *Ships That Made U. S. History*. New York: McGraw-Hill, 1950.

Mudra, Marie. *David Farragut*. New York: Messner, 1953.

Pratt, Fletcher. *Monitor and Merrimac*. New York: Random House, 1951.

Roscoe, Theodore, and Freeman, Fred. *Picture History of the U. S. Navy*. New York: Scribner's, 1956.

Snow, Dorothea. *John Paul Jones: Saltwater Boy*. Indianapolis: Bobbs-Merrill Co., Inc., 1950.

Sperry, Armstrong. *John Paul Jones, Fighting Sailor*. New York: Random House, 1953.

Strong, Charles S. *Story of American Sailing Ships*. New York: Grosset, 1957.

Tregaskis, Richard. *Guadalcanal Diary*. New York: Random House, 1955.

Wibberley, Leonard. *John Barry, Father of the Navy*. New York: Farrar, Straus, 1957.

BIBLIOGRAPHY

Alden, C. S., and Westcott, Allen. *The United States Navy*. Philadelphia: Lippincott, 1943.

Allen, Gardner W. *A Naval History of the American Revolution*. 2 vols. Boston: Houghton Mifflin, 1913.

Allen, Gardner W. *Our Naval War With France*. Boston: Houghton Mifflin, 1909.

Augur, Helen. *The Secret War of Independence*. New York: Duell, Sloan & Pearce, 1956.

Barrows, Edward M. *The Great Commodore; the Exploits of Matthew Calbraith Perry*. Indianapolis: Bobbs-Merrill, 1935.

Beach, Edward L. *Submarine!* New York: Henry Holt, 1952.

Beirne, Francis F. *The War of 1812*. New York: E. P. Dutton, 1949.

Buchanan, A. R. (ed.). *The Navy's Air War*. New York: Harper & Brothers, 1946.

Cant, Gilbert. *America's Navy in World War II*. New York: John Day, 1943.

Cope, Harley, and Karig, Walter. *Battle Submerged; Submarine Fighters of World War II*. New York: Norton, 1951.

Cross, Wilbur. *Challengers of the Deep*. New York: William Sloane Associates, 1959.

DeLong, George W. *The Voyage of the Jeanette. The Ship and Ice Journals of George W. DeLong, Lieutenant - Commander*. Boston: Houghton Mifflin, 1884.

Frost, Holloway H. *We Build A Navy*. Annapolis, Maryland: U. S. Naval Institute, 1929.

Frothingham, Thomas G. *The Naval History of the World War (The United States in the War, 1917-18, Vol. III)*. Cambridge: Harvard University Press, 1926.

Henry, Robert S. *The Story of the Mexican War*. Indianapolis: Bobbs-Merrill, 1950.

Jane's Fighting Ships. New York: McGraw-Hill.

King, Ernest J. *U. S. Navy at War: Official Reports to the Secretary of the Navy*. Washington, D. C.: U. S. Navy Department, 1946.

Knox, Dudley W. *A History of the United States Navy*. New York: G. P. Putnam, 1936.

Lewis, C. L. *Famous American Naval Officers*. Boston: L. C. Page, 1944.

Lockwood, Charles A. *Sink 'em All: Submarine Warfare in the Pacific*. New York: Dutton, 1951.

McEwen, W. A., and Lewis, A. H. *Encyclopedia of Nautical Knowledge*. Cambridge. Maryland: Cornell Maritime Press, 1953.

Mahan, A. T. *The Major Operations of the Navies in the War of American Independence*. Boston: Little Brown, 1913.

Mahan, A. T. *Sea Power in Its Relation to the War of 1812*. 2 vols. Boston: Little Brown, 1905.

Metcalf, Clyde H. *A History of the U. S. Marine Corps*. New York: Putnam, 1939.

Miller, Francis T. *The Photographic History of the Civil War (The Navies, Vol. VI)*. New York: Review of Reviews, 1911.

Millholland, Ray. *The Splinter Fleet of the Otranto Barrage*. Indianapolis: Bobbs-Merrill, 1936.

Mitchell, Donald W. *History of the Modern American Navy*. New York: Knopf, 1946.

Morison, Samuel Eliot. *History of the United States Naval Operations in World War II*. 14 vols. Boston: Little Brown, 1947-1960.

Noel, John. *Naval Terms Dictionary*. New York: D. Van Nostrand, 1952.

Official Records of the Union and Confederate Navies in the War of Rebellion. (Published under the direction of the Hon. George Meyer, Secretary of the Navy.) Washington: Government Printing Office,

Pratt, Fletcher. *Compact History of the United States Navy*. New York: Hawthorn, 1957.

Pratt, F. *The Navy: A History*. Garden City, N.Y.: Doubleday, Doran, 1938.

Roberts, W. A., and Brentano, Lowell (editors). *The Book of the Navy*. Garden City, New York: Doubleday, Doran, 1944.

Roscoe, Theodore, and Freeman, Fred (artist). *A Picture History of the United States Navy*. New York: Scribner's, 1956.

Roscoe, T. *United States Submarine Operations in World War II*. Annapolis: U. S. Naval Institute, 1949.

Sargent, Nathan (compiler). *Admiral Dewey and the Manila Campaign*. Washington: Naval Historical Foundation, 1947.

Sprout, Harold and Margaret. *The Rise of American Naval Power*. Princeton: Princeton University Press, 1942.

Westcott, Allan F. (ed.). *American Sea Power Since 1775*. Philadelphia: Lippincott, 1947.

Woodward, C. V. *The Battle for Leyte Gulf*. New York: Macmillan, 1947.

ACKNOWLEDGMENTS: The editors are deeply grateful to Rear Admiral John B. Heffernan, USN (Ret.) for giving generously of his knowledge of the history of the Navy and for his guidance and advice; and to Esther Cross and Tadd Fisher, who helped in researching the manuscript. In addition, they wish expressly to thank the following individuals and organizations for their generous assistance and cooperation in furnishing pictorial materials from their collections: Capt. F. Kent Loomis, USN (Ret.), Asst. Director of Naval History, Mr. Henry A. Vadnais, Naval History Div., and Mr. Charles Lawrence, Combat Art Div.—U.S. Navy Department; Mr. J. C. Van Hoozier—U. S. Naval Photographic Center; Ensign Thomas Little—Third Naval District, Capt. Wade DeWeese (Ret.), Director, and Miss Eleanor Donehoo—U. S. Naval Academy Museum, Annapolis; Dr. Philip Karl Lundeberg, Assoc. Curator—Div. of Naval History, Smithsonian Institution; Miss Virginia Daiker, Reference Librarian—Library of Congress; Mr. Herman Kahn, Director, and Mr. Raymond Corry—Franklin D. Roosevelt Library; Mrs. Thomas V. Brabrand, Curator of Prints—The Mariners Museum; Miss Dorothea C. Shipley—Old Print Shop; Mr. Irving S. Olds, New York City; Dr. S. W. Jackman, Bates College; Mr. John D. Schiff, New York City, Mr. Henry B. Beville, Washington, and Mr. J. Stuart Whelan, Jr., Annapolis—Photographers.

INDEX

Bold face indicates pages on which maps or illustrations appear

153

DAVID GLASGOW FARRAGUT

FLAG OF THE SECRETARY OF THE NAVY

M. C. PERRY'S FLAG, JAPAN, 1853.

A JAPANESE KAMIKAZE, OR SUICIDE PL

GEORGE DEWEY

TORPEDO SQUADRON 3

CRUISER SCOUTIN
SQUADRON 8